Extraordinary Praise for the *New York Times* Bestseller
What Paul Meant by Garry Wills

"Garry Wills is simultaneously one of this country's leading public intellectuals and American Catholicism's most formidable lay scholar. To find someone approaching his equal in both spheres, in fact, you would probably have to go back to the mid-nineteenth century and Rome's great convert from Transcendentalism, the abolitionist and champion of labor Orestes Brownson. . . . What makes Wills's contribution unique in a country whose shelves of religious books these days overflow with vitriol, bombast and treacle is his singular combination of intellectual integrity and authentically unsentimental spirituality. Read *What Paul Meant* to get a sense of what the preacher from Tarsus really intended—and for what Garry Wills has to offer us all."   —*Los Angeles Times*

"A tour-de-force revision of what we thought we knew about the apostle who helped give the Christian faith its distinctive shape."
—Slate.com

"Wills writes more gracefully and economically than scholarly authors in this gem of a book."   —*The Boston Globe*

"With this bracing book . . . [Wills] further cements his reputation as one of the most intellectually interesting and doctrinally heterodox Christians writing today."   —*The New York Times Book Review*

"With characteristic clarity and insight, Garry Wills has given us a vital study of the earliest voice of the New Testament. We can get no closer to Jesus than through the writings of Paul, and Wills's book expertly separates fact from fiction and history from legend, illuminating those epochal early years after the Passion. It is true, as Paul said, that we 'see through a glass, darkly,' but Wills has now helped us see the theology of the most important apostle much more clearly."
—Jon Meacham, editor of *Newsweek* and author of *American Gospel: God, the Founding Fathers, and the Making of a Nation*

"Everybody should be as lucky as St. Paul. Not only did he have a transformative spiritual experience and become a founder of one of the world's great religions, but two thousand years later he has Garry Wills to explain, interpret and defend him. . . . One could hardly wish for a more capable advocate than Wills."

—*Chicago Tribune*

"*What Paul Meant* is a scholarly reevaluation of the letters of Paul. Wills is a questioning Roman Catholic, and his arguments will surprise and challenge traditional views of Paul."

—*The Times Union* (Albany)

"Provocative yet helpful, this book is sure to create a buzz."

—*Publishers Weekly*

"I had realized for a long time that Saint Paul was the first of the New Testament writers, but I did not realize all the implications. Sociologically, this is the best description of how the Jesus movement emerged."

—Andrew M. Greeley, author of *The Catholic Revolution*

"*What Paul Meant* is a fascinating read, worth examining by anyone with an open mind and an interest in Christianity and its most prolific early voice."

—*St. Petersburg Times*

"Wills homes in on what is at stake in complex arguments, makes the issues clear, and presents a compelling case for reading Paul with historical attentiveness."

—*Library Journal*

"Lucid . . . Wills is not a biblical scholar, but he is a voracious reader and an eloquent writer who makes judicious use of the best recent scholarship."

—*The Washington Post*

"In this book, Wills displays his great gift for exposition. He can communicate enormously complex interpretive problems in astonishingly little space with great lucidity. . . . Erudite and engaging, slyly humorous and dead serious, scholarly and passionate."

—*The Christian Century*

PENGUIN BOOKS

WHAT PAUL MEANT

Garry Wills has written many acclaimed works on religion. His *What Jesus Meant, Papal Sin,* and *Why I Am a Catholic* were *New York Times* bestsellers. He studied for the priesthood, took his doctorate in the classics, and taught Greek for many years at the Johns Hopkins University. He is now Professor of History Emeritus at Northwestern University. His works on American history have received many awards, including the Pulitzer Prize for *Lincoln at Gettysburg.*

GARRY WILLS

What Paul Meant

PENGUIN BOOKS

PENGUIN BOOKS

Published by the Penguin Group

Penguin Group (USA) Inc., 375 Hudson Street, New York, New York 10014, U.S.A.
Penguin Group (Canada), 90 Eglinton Avenue East, Suite 700, Toronto,
Ontario, Canada M4P 2Y3 (a division of Pearson Penguin Canada Inc.)
Penguin Books Ltd, 80 Strand, London WC2R 0RL, England
Penguin Ireland, 25 St Stephen's Green, Dublin 2, Ireland
(a division of Penguin Books Ltd)
Penguin Group (Australia), 250 Camberwell Road, Camberwell,
Victoria 3124, Australia (a division of Pearson Australia Group Pty Ltd)
Penguin Books India Pvt Ltd, 11 Community Centre,
Panchsheel Park, New Delhi – 110 017, India
Penguin Group (NZ), 67 Apollo Drive, Rosedale, North Shore 0632,
New Zealand (a division of Pearson New Zealand Ltd)
Penguin Books (South Africa) (Pty) Ltd, 24 Sturdee Avenue,
Rosebank, Johannesburg 2196, South Africa

Penguin Books Ltd, Registered Offices:
80 Strand, London WC2R 0RL, England

First published in the United States of America by Viking Penguin,
a member of Penguin Group (USA) Inc. 2006
Published in Penguin Books 2007

ISBN 0-670-03793-1 (hc.)
ISBN 978-0-14-311263-1 (pbk.)
CIP data available

Set in Aldus   Designed by Francesca Belanger

146119709

TO THE CATHOLIC WORKERS

who know what Jesus meant

Contents

Introduction: "The Bad News Man" *1*

1. Paul and the Risen Jesus *19*

2. Paul and the Pre-Resurrection Jesus *39*

3. Paul "on the Road" *57*

4. Paul and Peter *73*

5. Paul and Women *89*

6. Paul and the Troubled Gatherings *105*

7. Paul and Jews *125*

8. Paul and Jerusalem *141*

9. Paul and Rome *157*

Afterword: Misreading Paul *171*

Appendix: Translating Paul 177

Acknowledgments 193

What Paul Meant

Introduction: "The Bad News Man"

✝

MANY PEOPLE THINK that Judas was the supreme betrayer of Jesus. But others say Paul has a better right to that title. Judas gave Jesus' body over to death. Paul, it is claimed, buried his spirit. He substituted his own high-flown but also dark theology for the simple teachings of the itinerant preacher from Galilee. Thomas Jefferson wrote to his friend William Short that Paul was the "first corrupter of the doctrines of Jesus." Bernard Shaw said the same thing in the preface to his play *Androcles and the Lion:* "There has never been a more monstrous imposition perpetrated than the imposition of the limitations of Paul's soul upon the soul of Jesus." This represented a triumph over the four evangelists ("good news bearers") by what Nietzsche called Paul in *The Antichrist*—"the Dysangelist" (Bad News Bearer), a man with "a genius for hatred." Shaw told a correspondent in 1928 that "it would have been better for the world if Paul had never been born."

What causes such harsh judgments on Paul? It is said he threw the human mind into prisons of sinful doom and predestination, subjecting human beings to a "law in their members," trapping them in "the flesh," so that neither moral effort nor religious code can free them from this bondage. Paul inspired pessimisms as influential as those of Augustine and Luther and Pascal (Nietzsche called Paul "the Jewish Pascal"). In line with such tidings of great gloom, Paul's letters have become the place to go, over the centuries, for attacks on women, marriage, gays, and Jews—especially Jews. The great German scholar Adolf von Harnack proclaimed—in *What Is Christianity?*—that Paul "confidently regarded the Gospel as a new force abolishing the religion of the [Jewish] Law." Jews, naturally, have been less than happy with that judgment, suspecting that the deep anti-Semitism of Christianity comes in large part from Paul. The attitude of some Jews, complained Richard Rubenstein, can be summed up as "Jesus, yes; Paul, never!"[1]

The Outsider

HOW WAS PAUL able to subvert, so early and so thoroughly, the message of Jesus? Those who believe he did so can argue that he was bound to, since there was no reason for him to know or understand Jesus, a figure he never met. In fact, during the earthly career of Jesus, Paul was never in the same country with him. Jesus came from Judaea and never moved outside it. Paul came from Cilicia (specifically, from Tarsus) and became a follower of Jesus in Syria (specifically, Damascus). Paul did not even go to Judaea for three years after he professed allegiance to Jesus, and he remained there for only two weeks. After this first visit, he stayed away for another fourteen years (Gal 2.1). He was, by his own account, not even recognizable there: "I was not known by my features *(prosōpon)* to the Judaean gatherings in Messiah" (Gal 1.22). Even when he tried to prove that he was a Jew among Jews, he did not claim Judaean birth or upbringing (Phil 3.4–6). In fact, he often took occasion to stress how distant he was, how independent, from the gatherings in Jerusalem.

Then how could Paul know much about what Jesus did or said in the land where he was born and lived? In fact, Paul's letters have few explicit mentions of Jesus' acts or words on earth. His acquaintance with the Jewish homeland being small, he concentrates on the risen Jesus, who appeared to him in the Diaspora. That is where, according to his critics, he picked up the components he would weave together into a new religion, reflecting his own psychological makeup and Greek education more than the rich events unfolded in the life of Jesus. The great scripture scholar Rudolf Bultmann wrote that "the teaching of the historical Jesus plays no role, or practically none, in Paul . . . in fact, his letters barely show any traces of the influence of the Palestinian tradition concerning the history and preaching of Jesus."[2]

With no credentials for knowing Jesus outside his own

private revelations, Paul dared to disagree with and criticize the original Twelve; and Peter, their leader; and James the brother of the Lord, who presided over the gathering in Jerusalem. He called Peter a hypocrite, one of those "who maintained a pretense" and "did not hew to the clearly marked meaning of the revelation" (Gal 2.13–14). He defended himself against "a party of Peter" in Corinth (1 Cor 1.12). He thought Peter had been misled by James (Gal 2.12) and he refers to the two of them as "apparent pillars" of the gathering in Jerusalem (Gal 2.9).

As befits one setting up his own religion, Paul became—in the eyes of early critics—"the father of heresies." All through Christian history Paul has been a sign of division, a stone on which many stumble. Apocryphal writings by Peter and James would charge Paul, in the second century, with being a tool of Satan. On the other side, Marcionites from that period claimed that only Paul and the Pauline "Luke" were authentically inspired authors. This kind of conflict was extended into the medieval use of Paul by various "antinomians." The problem reached its climax in the Reformation, a fight over what Paul meant in which, at times, there seemed to be little concern over what Jesus meant. It was not enough, then, for some to claim with Wilhelm Wrede that Paul was "the second founder of Christianity," second only to Jesus. He became the *only* founder of Christianity, leaving the misunderstood Jesus without any religion of his own.

The Letters

WHAT MADE PAUL such an apple of discord? The problem has its origin in his own words. It is sometimes said that the historical Jesus is hard to find because he left no writings of his own. Paul is hard to find precisely because he did leave writings. The letters attributed to him in the canonical New Testament seem to fall apart in our hands as we try to read them. Almost half of them (six of the thirteen) are no longer accepted by the mass of scholars as authentically his. Even some of the seven genuine ones are called composites, made up of several letters (or parts of letters), since they contradict one another or even themselves.[3] One or more letters may have been added after a first one on a papyrus roll, and then all recopied as a single letter when the rolls were recopied. Our seven genuine letters may thus be an amalgam of anywhere from eight to a dozen letters (or parts of letters). There are, besides, lost letters that Paul explicitly refers to or readers plausibly surmise. There may have been many earlier letters, written before Paul became so well known, before his network of correspondents increasingly saw the worth of what he wrote ("His letters, they say, are impressive and strong," 2 Cor 10.10), and before communities took care to preserve their own archives. There were probably later letters suppressed or destroyed because they were an embarrassment to the gatherings—whence the blackout on Paul's later days and death. So we have a spotty collection of writings, with many a known or unknown gap.

Even when one winnows down the few extant missives to an agreed-on authentic core, the letters remain dark or elusive. Within half a century or so of their composition, the "Peter" of the New Testament was calling them difficult and potentially misleading on the subject of the end time.

> Keep in mind that our rescue comes from the Lord's staying with us, as Paul, the brother we love, wrote to you out of the wisdom imparted to him. He has made the same point in all the letters he wrote on this subject. There are things in them hard to understand, which the unlettered and unsteady twist about—as with the rest of his writings—to their private and pernicious sense. (2 Pet 3.15–16)

It is not surprising that people should have trouble reading the letters of Paul. They are occasional writings, fired off to deal with local crises. He dictated them in the midst of various struggles, often to answer problems or refute opponents not clearly specified in his responses. We hear his raised voice without knowing what the other side was shouting. Some of the acerbic terms he uses were echoed back against now-invisible critics who first used them. Wayne Meeks rightly says: "We never see pure Pauline thought being developed at leisure by its own inner logic; rather, we see Paul always thinking under pressure, usually in the heat of immediate controversy."[4] The result is sometimes a lava flow of heated language, words tumbling out in self-defense or urgent exhortation. Paul is not a cool and remote philosopher but an embattled messenger—at times, as Nietzsche said, "disagreeable to himself and to others." He is a mystic and a deep theologian, but also a voluble street fighter, a man busy on many fronts, often harried, sometimes exasperated. To take on Paul is to plunge into a melee, as Donald Harman Akenson emphasizes:

> Saul, as revealed in his letters, was a feral creature. He would appear in one town or city after another, sometimes leaving footprints the size of craters, at other times, no marks at all, save a half-sentence in a later letter as the only mark of his coming and going. To the historical observer he is maddening, for he appears when least expected and he ducks out of sight just when we think he will be most useful.[5]

Keeping up with this theological Scarlet Pimpernel can be a strenuous endeavor. To quote Akenson again:

> At times, Saul reminds one of a vice-principal of a large urban high school who has to teach a daily class in calculus to the college-bound stream, then, as head of discipline he

breaks up a fight in the hall, and next he finds he has to fill in for a shop teacher who has gone home with a migraine. After school he coaches the offensive line of the football team, and finally at night he has to appear before a special session of the city council and give a polished argument for continued funding of the art and music classes. So we honor the canon of Saul's letters by accepting their sometimes-distracted, sometimes-staccato quality as part of the warrant of their authenticity, the words of a man on a mission.[6]

As one would expect of a man facing in so many directions to cope with so many tasks, Paul treated different situations with different approaches. He had to keep explaining his different treatment of Jesus' followers who were circumcised and those who were not. He gave different advice on observance of the Jewish food code to the Galatians and to the Romans. He refused to accept financial support from the Corinthians but welcomed it from the Galatians. He is frank about the flexibility of his mission strategies:

> While I am not anyone's slave, I have made myself everyone's slave, to win over more of them. For Jews I have been a Jew, to win over Jews. For those observing the Law I have been under the Law, though not subject to it, to win over those under the Law. To those free of the Law I have been free of the Law—not in fact free of God's law, but

under Messiah's law—to win over those free of the Law. I am weak with the weak, to win over the weak. To all people I am all things, so I may in all ways rescue some of them. All I do, I do for the sake of the revelation, that I may act along with the revelation. (1 Cor 9.19–23)

He gives plausible reasons (as we shall see) for these and other twists and turns. But their variety does not make him easy to follow.

The Best Witness

NO WONDER many people would just as soon avoid Paul's psychodrama and go "back" to the pure Gospels, which do not argue about understanding Jesus but just present him. Taking that shortcut was the obvious thing to do in the Middle Ages, when it was thought that the Gospels were written by the original followers of Jesus, who were eyewitnesses to what they set down. This led to the view that there was a primitive church, true to Jesus' simple teachings, which was later contaminated by Paul's doubts and theories and wrangling. (This is the Thomas Jefferson thesis.) But scholarly enquiry has destroyed the idea that the Gospels have a simple biographical basis. They are sophisticated theological constructs, none written by their putative authors, all drawing on second- or third- or fourth-hand accounts—and *all written from a quarter of a century to half a century after Paul's letters.* If we want to see what the original Jesus communities looked like, the first and best witness to this is Paul, the earliest writer of what would become in time the New Testament. In fact, his authentic letters are the only parts of the New Testament of which we can say that we know who wrote them. The Gospels, coming later, try to make sense of a history that already contained the conflicts Paul reveals to us. Those who believe in a providential revelation through the New Testament must deal with the fact that Providence preserved the first batch of inspired writings with the signature of Paul. His letters were written roughly two decades after the death of Jesus. Other New Testament letters attributed to Paul or to other authors (Peter, James, and John) are written two to five decades after his, and imitate the forms of his.

It was Paul who brought the good news to many communities. He still brings it to us. I shall argue that what Paul meant was not something other than or contrary to what Jesus meant, but that we can best find out the latter by studying the former. His letters stand closer to Jesus than do any other words in the New Testament. They were the first to be penned, the first to be saved. That fact must be remembered when we look at the Acts of the Apostles, the work of someone calling himself Luke. That book describes the travels and teachings of Paul, integrating them into the activities of other early members of the Jesus movement. The letters used to be interpreted in terms of the chronology and issues discussed in Acts. But that later account is often at odds with the earlier and authentic letters—for a very good reason. Luke does not cite or refer to any of the letters. In fact, *he does not seem to know they exist*. If he does, he treats them as a nuisance best ignored. That in itself is enough to destroy the image "Luke" presents of having known Paul, and even of having traveled or worked with him.

There are other grounds for treating Acts with great caution when it purports to be telling the story of Paul. Luke is writing after the Romans destroyed the Temple in Jerusalem (70 CE), a catastrophe that was still decades off when Paul wrote. Luke's contemporaries are trying to work out the troubled relations with their parent body of Jews, the displaced worshipers from the Temple and in the synagogues. With Luke and his contemporaries, there is the beginning of a separate church with a primitive because inchoate structure, in which various communities are becoming connected in a more systematic way. This proto-church is a body to which people are being converted, and Luke treats Paul as one of them. He also presents him as part of the Jerusalem community before it was dispersed, in accord with Luke's unifying program. He makes Paul's career show many good relations with Rome—he even makes Paul a Roman citizen—and he presents Paul's relations with Jews who do not believe in Jesus as more hostile than they are in the letters. That reflects the bitter circumstances of Luke's own traumatized time, the time when the Jews' world was upended with the obliteration of the Temple.

Luke's situation was not that of Paul. Paul never thinks of himself as a convert to some new religion. He preaches the Jewish God, Yahweh, and the Jewish Messiah. He preaches in synagogues. When he brings others to believe in Jesus, he teaches them from the Jewish holy writings, which were the only "Bible" of the day—his letters would not be joined together with later documents to create a separate "New Testament" till long after his death. Though relations between Jews who believed in Jesus and those who did not were becoming strained and even combative in Paul's time, he says there can be no permanent break. History is moving fast toward its conclusion, and the only conclusion he recognizes is the one God has arranged for his covenanted people. "Has God rejected his own people? Far from it" (Rom 11.1).

[Rather than thinking God had rejected his people] I could prefer to be outcast from Messiah myself if it would help my brothers, the forebears of my flesh, who are the Israelites. Theirs is the sonship, and the splendor, and the covenants and the gift of the Law, the rites, and the promises. From them are the patriarchs, and from them, by fleshly descent is the Messiah, the God above all, be he forever praised. (Rom 9.3–5)

Other peoples are to be included in God's final plan, but the original people cannot be excluded. How this was to happen was mysterious, but Paul and his fellow believers in the Diaspora were hurriedly trying to work the matter out. We shall see that he was not alone in his efforts, or the first to set up communities of believers in Jesus throughout the Diaspora. He worked from pre-existing bases, learning from and teaching his fellow emissaries of the Lord. Even when he arrives in cities new to him, he often meets and works with fellow believers from Rome and elsewhere, places that already had "gatherings in Jesus," as he put it.

All of this is hard to understand if we go back to Paul through later assumptions with a familiar (but anachronistic) framework. That is why this book will forswear the use of terms for things that did not exist in Paul's world—terms like *church* or *Christians, priests* or *sacraments.* (For reaching back to Paul's "pre-churchy" language, see my Appendix.) When Paul addresses the *ekklesiai,* the "gatherings in Jesus," he is writing to those who met in the homes of particular men or women, in the same town or in several towns. He addresses himself to the whole gathering, in each case, not to some leader or leaders. Some towns had more than one such home-gathering. There was no hierarchy among the gatherings, one having more authority over another. The housekeepers, whether male or female or both, were the informal leaders of the gathering. Emissaries—for this sense of *apostle,* see my

Appendix—moved from gathering to gathering, normally in teams, often husband-and-wife teams (Rom 16.6–15), like the team of Peter and his wife, or of the Lord's brothers and their wives (1 Cor 9.5). Paul usually had several partners in his team—most of his letters are written with cosenders, and he often refers to coworkers, women as well as men.

New gatherings were hived off from pre-existing ones, sometimes by the work of emissaries like Paul's team, sometimes by the gathering's own natural reach outward toward friends or relatives or associates, either in the same town or in other ones. The proliferation of these gatherings was astonishingly rapid. They had grown out from Palestine even before Paul came to believe in Jesus. They were already present in the country where he was living (Syria). He began his work as a junior partner (with Barnabas) in an emissary team operating from a pre-existing gathering at Antioch. The story of Paul is never that of an individual, some religious genius hatching his own religion out of his own head. We find in his letters hymns that communities had formed and sung before he set them down in an epistle. He constantly appeals to traditions handed on to him, to be handed on to others. It is as a testimony to the vital explosion of belief in Jesus all across the Diaspora that Paul assumes his importance.

He takes us closer in time to Jesus than does any other person or group or body of writings. The best way to find out what Jesus meant to his early followers is to see what Paul meant to his fellow believers, many of whom had seen Jesus in his earthly lifetime or after his Resurrection, without having written their stories down for us. Paul did write. But he was writing about a shared experience, not a single and idiosyncratic one. If Paul was such a foe and underminer of Jesus, why was he accepted so soon and broadly by those who knew Jesus? The answer is that Paul was not a counterforce to Jesus but one of the early believers who together bore witness to him. The Jesus gatherings in the Diaspora proved more fertile and lasting than those in Judaea itself, not because of any one man's brilliance, energy, or deceptions, but because they were more vitally expressive of what Jesus meant. Paul was part of this explosion of belief. His letters are dispatches from that hurricane of activity.

The Pauline Writings

THIRTEEN LETTERS are attributed to Paul in the New Testament, and for centuries they were all accepted as his. But modern scholarship has reached a consensus that some were definitely not written by him and others are of dubious authenticity. Only seven are now accepted as certainly by him. The seven in their probable order of composition are

1 Thess   Letter to the Thessalonians
Gal   Letter to the Galatians

Phil	Letter to the Philippians
Phlm	Letter to Philemon
1 Cor	First Letter to the Corinthians
2 Cor	Second Letter to the Corinthians
Rom	Letter to the Romans

Two letters seem to be written by followers of Paul who had a profound understanding of what could be made of his teaching:

Col	Letter to the Colossians
Eph	Letter to the Ephesians

One letter seems a clumsy restatement of a genuine one:

2 Thess	Purported Letter to the Thessalonians

Three later letters are written in circumstances and from standpoints clearly not Paul's:

Tit	Letter to Titus
1 Tim	First Letter to Timothy
2 Tim	Second Letter to Timothy

For understanding what Paul meant, one must rely on the letters accepted by almost all scholars as authentic. This book will use only those seven letters.

NOTES

1. Richard L. Rubenstein, *My Brother Paul* (Harper & Row, 1972), p. 114.

2. Rudolf Bultmann, *Theology of the New Testament*, translated by Kentrick Grobel (Scribner, 1955), pp. 35, 188.

3. It is widely agreed that the Second Letter to the Corinthians combines two separate missives, and some find as many as six original components tucked into it. Two letters are also found in the First Letter to the Thessalonians and the First Letter to the Corinthians, while three or more have been found in the Letter to the Romans. Thus the seven authentic writings of Paul may be made up of a dozen or more works by him.

4. Wayne A. Meeks, *The Writings of St. Paul* (W. W. Norton & Company, 1972), p. 438.

5. Donald Harman Akenson, *Saint Saul: A Skeleton Key to the Historical Jesus* (Oxford University Press, 2000), p. 129.

6. Ibid., p. 134.

1. Paul and the Risen Jesus

✝

THE MOST IMPORTANT EVENT of Paul's life, that which determined everything else, was his encounter with the risen Jesus. He puts this in a social context, as part of the Resurrection experience that other followers of Jesus shared. His own account of this epochal occurrence does not accord with the most famous story of Paul's "conversion," that given in the Acts of the Apostles (9.1–9). But that story, told by one "Luke," was written half a century after what it purports to describe, and we shall find that it has many holes in it. Here are Paul's own words, close to the event:

> My urgent concern was to pass on to you what was passed on to me—that Christ died for our sins, in accord with the sacred writings, that he was buried, that he arose on the third day, in accord with the sacred writings, that he appeared to Kephas, then to the Twelve. After that, he appeared at the same time to more than five hundred of the Brothers, most of whom are still with us, though some have died. And after that he appeared to James, then to all the emissaries.[1] Finally, as by a delayed birth, he appeared to me, though I am the least of the emissaries, one

not even worthy to be called an emissary, since I persecuted God's gathering. (1 Cor 15.3–9)

Paul puts his own experience in the context of the Gospel revelation, of the tradition passed on to him, which it is his urgent concern to pass on to others, in company with the other
emissaries, his superiors.

The principal thing to notice here is that Jesus *appeared* to
Paul—*ōphthē*, "he was *seen*." In Luke's account of Paul's encounter with Jesus, Paul sees nothing—a sudden flash of light
proves literally blinding, so that he merely hears a voice. This
is technically not an apparition but a *photism* (a light flash)
accompanied by an *audition* (a disembodied voice). In the
Gospel stories of meetings with the risen Jesus, genuine ap-
paritions occur—the Lord not only appears to men and
women but he converses with those who see him, he gives instructions, he answers questions.[2] Paul, putting his own
record along with theirs, implies that his experience was like
theirs—that he spoke with Jesus. That is the credential he offers to others who also possess it. He asks to be tested by all
those he has identified as his fellow witnesses to the risen
Lord. "Am I not an emissary? *Have I not seen Jesus our
Lord?*" (1 Cor 9.1). That is why he can report that he had his
calling as an emissary to the nations directly from Jesus: "I,
Paul, made an emissary not in any human way, or through

any man, but through Jesus-Messiah and his Father, God, who raised him from the dead" (Gal 1.1).

Of all those who saw the risen Lord, Paul is the only one whose own words we possess. The other accounts are second- or third- or fourth-hand, written down four or five decades after the Resurrection. Yet Paul, at the time he wrote, met many of those who shared his privilege—people who could have challenged his claim. No doubt he shared his own story with them, they all "compared notes."

And of all this large company of witnesses to the Resurrection, only Paul has described (so far as that is possible) what a risen body is like. The others remark on an elusive or uncanny aspect to their encounters. They often do not at first recognize Jesus. He seems paradoxically physical (eating food) yet ghostly (gliding through a door), ordinary (a gardener, a traveler) yet transfigured.[3] Paul, who knows what he is talking about, says that the risen body does not fit any of our expectations. Only he, of those who have seen such a body, tells us what it is like:

> Will someone ask, in what way are the dead raised, and in what kind of body do they fare? Do not be a fool. Even a seed you sow does not come to life until it dies. And what you sow is not the plant it will become; it is a mere seed—of wheat, perhaps, or of some other grain. God

gives it the plant he has decreed, a different plant according to what seed is sown. And all flesh is not the same, but that of humans, or of beasts, or of birds, or of fish. There are, moreover, heavenly bodies and earthly bodies, and the splendor of the heavenly bodies is one thing, the splendor of earthly bodies another. There is one splendor for the sun, another for the moon, and another for the stars—since star from star differs in splendor.

That is how it is with the resurrection of the dead. Sown in disintegration, it is raised in integrity. Sown in disgrace, it is raised in splendor. Sown in frailty, it is raised in strength. What is sown as a sensate body is raised as a spiritual body. If there is a sensate body, there is also a spiritual body. For it is written: "The first man, Adam, became a living soul." But the last Adam became a life-giving spirit. Yet the spiritual comes not first; rather the sensate is first, and then the spiritual. The first man came from the clay of earth; the second came from heaven. As the first man was of clay, so are the others claylike. And as the last man was from heaven, so are all his fellows heavenly. And as we have borne the likeness of the man of clay, so shall we bear the likeness of the man from heaven.

So, brothers, I assure you, flesh and blood cannot have any inheritance in God's reign, any more than disintegration can have any inheritance in integrity. That is the secret thing I am telling you. Though we all may not die, we shall all be altered at a stroke, at an eyeblink, at a last trumpet blast, and the dead will awaken in integrity and we shall be altered. Then must disintegration be clothed in integrity, and death be clothed in deathlessness. When such death is clothed in deathlessness, the word will apply: Death, what victory have you? What stab, Death, is left you? (1 Cor 15.35–55)

Paul inevitably associated what other risen bodies would be like from his encounter with that of Jesus. "He will transfigure our body's lowliness into the pattern of his dazzling body" (Phil 3.21). "By looking with unveiled faces at the glory of the Lord mirrored back on us, we are transformed into that image, from splendor to splendor, by the working of the Lord's Spirit" (2 Cor 3.18). When Paul talks of seeing the splendor of Jesus' face, it is often assumed or asserted that he is registering the internal assent of faith, but there is no reason we should artificially keep his statement apart from his report that he had actually seen the Lord's face: "The God who said, 'Let light shine out of the dark,' has shone a light in our heart to understand the splendor of God that is the features *(prosōpon)* of Messiah" (1 Cor 4.6). Paul is our expert on the risen body, and he shows a fascination with it. He writes about the longing for it.

When this transitory housing we inhabit is dissolved, we know another housing is prepared for us by God, a lasting casement in the heavens not made by hand. We naturally chafe in our present casing, yearning for the heavenly one to be put on over it, lest we be caught naked but for our first habiliment—we chafe while pent in this narrow enclosure, though not wanting to put it off until it is enclosed in the new casing, so that the mortal shall be absorbed into the immortal. God has prompted us to this yearning, and has given us the Spirit as a surety of its fulfillment. Bracing ourselves on all sides, then, realizing that while we are held in by our bodies we are held off from the Lord, we fare on, believing beyond what we see, bracing ourselves as I say and taking heart to leave the body's home and enter the Lord's home, making it our point of pride to win his favor, however disembodied or re-embodied. (2 Cor 5.1–9)

Paul is attributing to others his own yearning to be freed into the higher state where Jesus has led the way. "For me, living is Christ and dying a boon. . . . I feel an urgency for dissolution, to be with Christ" (Phil 1.21, 23).

The tug between the present body and what he had seen of the future one played into Paul's mystical experience of prayer. This is something he would not have mentioned in his letters had Corinthian spiritualists not boasted of their ecstatic states as a warrant for their aberrations. Paul refutes their arguments, but also says that such experiences do not excuse their conduct. He is a bit embarrassed at having to engage in such competitive spiritual credentialing, so he modestly puts his claim in the third person.

> I am forced to boast. Though it does me little good, I will venture on the subject of visions and revelations from the Lord. I know a man in Messiah who, fourteen years ago—whether in his body or out of it I know not, God knows—was swept up high as the third heaven. And I know that this very man—whether in his body or out of it, I know not—was swept up into Paradise, where he heard unspeakable words, words it is impossible for a man to pronounce. About such a man I might boast, but about myself I may boast only of weaknesses. (2 Cor 12.1–5)

Apparently describing the same time, he assured the glossolalists of Corinth: "Thank God I can speak in tongues more than all of you—though I would rather speak five intelligible words in the gathering, to be understood by others, than speak thousands of words in tongues" (1 Cor 14.18–19).

By dating his ecstasies back to a specific time, Paul no doubt refers to the key period in his life, that in which he received his call from Jesus. As soon as Jesus appeared to him, he went to Arabia—to the desert just over the eastern border of Syria (the country Damascus is in).

> I would have you know, Brothers, that the revelation I revealed to you came not in the ordinary human way, for I

did not receive it from a man by way of teaching. Rather, it was directly revealed to me by Jesus-Messiah. For you have heard how I led my life under the Jewish Law, that I was extreme in my persecution of God's gathering, trying to extirpate it, how I surpassed many of my contemporaries in adherence to Jewish Law, more highly devoted to the traditions I received from the ancestors. But when the time came for what God had destined me to from the womb, summoning me by his favor, he directly revealed his Son to me, that I might proclaim him to the nations. At this point I consulted no flesh-and-blood person. Nor did I go to Jerusalem, to see emissaries called before me. I went off, instead, to Arabia, whence I later returned to Damascus. (Gal 1.11–17)

Why would Paul go even farther off from Jerusalem—to Arabia? Some have said he was acting at once on the commission to preach to "the nations." But that underestimates the wrenching experience that turned him from a fierce assault on "the Brothers" as enemies of the Law. He had to come to grips with all his earlier misconceptions. He had to reconcile somehow his reading of Jewish destiny and its improbable fulfillment in Jesus as Messiah. We also have to suppose that Jesus, in his appearance to him, directed Paul toward a kind of desert experience of intense prayer and study. All the later citations of the sacred writings that Paul made while dictating his letters "on the road" could not have come from ad hoc unrolling of the bulky papyruses of the Bible. He had to puzzle out, under divine guidance, where he had been wrong in his reading of the prophets, what new light was cast on them by the words Jesus spoke to him. This deep involvement let him quote scripture extensively from memory (it is noticed that he is often slightly "off" the precise wording). There is no reason to suppose that Jesus appeared to him only once. He appeared to others several times and in several places (Mt 28.10, Jn 21.1). In fact, Paul tells us of a later apparition (Gal 2.2), when he decided to go to Jerusalem, not summoned or sent by men, but "directed by an apparition" (*apokalypsis,* the same word he uses of Jesus' apparition to him at Gal 1.12 and 1.16).

Paul, by withdrawing into Arabia, away from his home and prior associations, was able to develop what would continue to be his passionate intimacy with Jesus. "It is no longer I who live—Messiah lives in me" (Gal 2.20). "It is in Messiah-Jesus that I take pride for service to God, though I dare not say this is anything but Jesus himself working through me to bring the nations to his service" (Rom 15.17–18). "I made up my mind not to display any learning to you, only Messiah, and him as crucified" (1 Cor 2.2). "Be imitators of me, as I am of Messiah" (1 Cor 11.1). "I bear on my body Jesus' wounds" (Gal 6.17). Paul's identification with Jesus was not just a personal matter. It was what he saw as the essence of belief for all his Brothers. This is what made them "the Holy," the persons "in Jesus." Baptism had incorporated them into the Messianic fulfillment of history. "We were buried with him by this baptism into his death, so that, just as Messiah rose from the dead to the splendor of his Father, we should fare forward in a life entirely new" (Rom 6.3–4). "Anyone in Messiah is a new order of being, the ancient things have passed away, and—see!—the new ones begin" (2 Cor 5.17).

In Paul's dizzying early days of communication with Jesus, he had to reconcile his earlier devotion to the Jewish Law with his experience of the risen Jesus—and he came to recognize the latter as the fulfillment of the former. Jesus is the Promised One: "Messiah is the Law's completion" (Rom 10.4). In most English translations of Paul's letters, "Christ" is taken as a name, not a title. "Jesus Christ" is made to sound like a full name (praenomen and cognomen). But *Khristos* in Greek is a title, like *Kyrios* (Lord). It is the Greek form of Hebrew "Messiah." Both words mean "Anointed." Paul sometimes refers to Jesus as the Messiah, or just Messiah, or Jesus-Messiah, or Messiah-Jesus. But it is always his *title* that is at stake, and we should keep this as much to the forefront of our minds as it was to his, since it is what unites the risen Jesus with his Jewish destiny.[4] That is why the basic revelation of faith for Paul was always that Jesus died for our sins and rose again, *in accord with the sacred writings* (1 Cor 15.3–4).

The experience of the risen Jesus was not only the pivotal event in Paul's own life. It was for him the center of salvation history, for the Jews and for the world. It is what he preaches.

Without it, he would have nothing to say and the gatherings would have nothing to bring them into existence.

> If it is our revelation that Messiah was raised from the dead, how can some of you say that there is no resurrection from the dead? If there is no resurrection from the dead, how could Messiah have been raised? If Messiah was not raised, our revelation is an empty thing, as is your faith, and we are guilty of false testimony about God, since we were God's witnesses that he had raised Messiah, which he could not have done if the dead cannot be raised. If in fact the dead are not raised, the Messiah was not raised; and if Messiah was not raised, your faith is pointless, and you are still in sin's thrall. More that that, those who died in Messiah have simply perished. If our hope in Messiah is only for this present life, we are the most pitiable of all human beings. But Messiah truly was raised, the first harvest of all who die. As death came through one man, so resurrection comes through one man. (1 Cor 15.12–21)

He cannot repeat this message of the Resurrection often or urgently enough.

> We look toward his Son's appearance from the heavens, the one he raised from the dead, Jesus our rescuer from the impending wrath. (1 Thess 1.10)

[I am] an emissary from Jesus-Messiah, and from God his Father, who raised him from the dead. (Gal 1.1)

. . . to experience him and the energy of his Resurrection and the oneness with his sufferings, shaping myself to the pattern of his death, to have a share in his Resurrection from the dead. (Phil 3.10–11)

. . . knowing that he who raised Jesus the Lord will raise us along with him, and bring us to his side. (2 Cor 4.14)

Baptized into Messiah-Jesus, we were baptized into his death. We were buried with him by this baptism into his death, so that, just as Messiah rose from the dead to the splendor of his Father, so we may fare forward in a life entirely new. (Rom 6.3–4)

Luke's Story

IT IS IMPORTANT to get Paul's own words firmly in mind when considering his relation to the risen Jesus, since—as has already been mentioned—his own version is not the famous one. That comes from the Acts of the Apostles, and it is so sensational that there can be no wonder that it has eclipsed his own words. The Acts of the Apostles has been called a theological novel, and it does share some traits with the Hellenistic novels being written at the same time as Acts—wandering preachers, miracles, sea adventures, long rhetorical speeches.

The story of Paul's "conversion" is so good that the author of Acts repeats it three times, each time with variations. In one version, bystanders fall down when Paul does (Ac 26.14). In another, they stay standing (9.7). In one, the bystanders see a light, but hear no voice (22.9). In another, they hear a voice but see nothing (9.7). In short, in one version people get the photism without the audition, in the other one they get the audition without the photism—but Paul, Luke assures us, got them both. By the third version, what the voice says is considerably expanded in length as well as intention (26.16–18).

Luke is a theological artist. He creates for a purpose, and the purpose can shift from one part of his story to the next. He wrote the Gospel that bears his name, and the beautiful accounts he created of Jesus' birth and presentation in the Temple, with their accompanying canticles, show how good he was at presenting doctrine as narrative. His theological purpose in dealing with Paul will be considered later, but the first thing to note about his accounts is their distance not only from Paul's words but from legal possibility and historical probability. The best known of the three versions is the first one in the book. Paul had already appeared in Jerusalem as Saul (his Hebrew name), where Luke says he was a student of the great Pharisee scholar Gamaliel (Ac 22.3). Though Gamaliel was known to oppose zealots, Saul joined the hotheads who stoned Stephen, the first martyr for Jesus. He kept the executioners' coats as he condoned their violence (Ac 7.57). Not content with that, Saul decided to go and do likewise, first in Judaea: "Saul raided the gathering, going house to house, dragging men and women off to prison" (Ac 8.3). Then he moved out to a foreign land:

Saul, snorting even greater threats of murder against the Lord's followers, went to the high priest with a request for letters to the synagogues in Damascus, to identify those of the Path, male or female, and bring them back in chains to Jerusalem. But as he neared Damascus, a sudden flash from heaven lightened all about him, and he heard a voice as he fell to the ground, saying, "Saul, Saul, why are you persecuting me?" And he asked, "Who, Lord, are you?" And he: "I am Jesus, the one you are persecuting. But get up and go into the town, and you will be told what you must do." His companions on the trip had stood there speechless, hearing a voice but seeing no one. Saul then got up from the ground but, on opening his eyes, was able to see nothing. So they led him by the hand into town. For three days he saw nothing, nor did he eat or drink.

There was a follower in Damascus named Ananias, and to him the Lord called, "Ananias," in a vision. He responded, "Here, Lord." And the Lord said: "Get up and go to Straight Street, and look for a man named Saul of Tarsus in the house of Judas. He is praying there, you see, since he has seen in a vision one called Ananias coming to lay hands on him and restore his sight." But Ananias said, "Lord, many people have told me about this man, all the suffering he has brought on your Holy Ones in Jerusalem, and that he has a mandate from the high priests to arrest all who call upon your name." The Lord told him: "Off with you, this is the instrument I have fitted for carrying my name to the nations, to kings, and to Israel's sons, and I will make clear to him what he must suffer for that name of mine."

So Ananias went and entered the house, and said as he put hands on him, "Saul, Brother, the Lord has sent me—Jesus, who appeared to you on the road as you traveled—so that you may see again and be filled with the Holy Spirit. And instantly what seemed like scales fell from his eyes, and he could see. He rose and was baptized, and ate and became strong. (Ac 9.1–19)

The problems with this account are many.

1. We know from Paul that he was "not known by my features to the Judaean gatherings in Messiah" (Gal 1.22). How could that be, if he had been a student in Jerusalem of the high-profile Pharisee scholar Gamaliel? More important, how could a man who had gone house to house arresting the Brothers be unknown to them?

2. If Paul had been a pupil of the famous Gamaliel, he would surely have said so when he boasted of his Pharisaical training (Gal 1.14, Phil 3.5).

3. The role Luke assigns to the otherwise unknown Ananias, here made Paul's sponsor in the faith though Paul never mentions him, is directly contradicted by Paul's own words about the appearance of Jesus to him: "At this point I consulted no flesh-and-blood person" (Gal 1.16). Luke is just as much at odds with this passage: "I would have you know, Brothers, that the revelation I revealed to you came not in the ordinary human way, for I did not receive it from a man by way of teaching. Rather, it was directly revealed to me by Jesus-Messiah (Gal 1.11–12).

4. Jerusalem was under Roman occupation, and the authorities did not like to have religious fanatics stirring up trouble. Why would they let Saul go around "snorting threats of murder" and hauling people out of their houses? Why would the Brothers not draw the Romans' attention to their plight? Luke does not present the Romans as hostile to Christians.

5. How was Paul able to force his way into homes and kidnap people? Luke seems to imagine that he used Temple police for the task, but he is evasive on the actual commissioning of terrorism. In line with his generally hostile attitude to the Jews, he says in one place that the high priest sanctioned Paul's campaign (Ac 9.2). But elsewhere he attributes it to the Sanhedrin (Ac 22.5). Still again, it is the body of chief priests who are behind him (Ac 26.12).

6. More to the point, Jews under the occupation were not allowed to put men to death. That is why Jesus had to be turned over to the Romans for execution (Jn 18.31).[5] Yet Luke later puts these words in Paul's mouth: "I not only put many of the Holy in prison, under orders from the chief priests, but I voted for their death sentences" (Ac 26.10). If the Jews had been able to execute men (and they were not), only the Sanhedrin could have carried out the sentence, and the idea that Paul was a member of the Sanhedrin is absurd. (Remember, he was not even known by his features in Judaea.)

7. To cap all the other impossibilities, the high priest could not have authorized Paul to search out and arrest people *in another country*. Damascus was in Syria, whose Roman rulers would hardly recognize an authority that was not even valid in Judaea. The archpriest would want to avoid trouble with the Romans, not court it by challenges to the peace. Saul could not have kidnapped masses of people from a foreign authority.

8. Finally, since Luke has improbably brought Paul down to Judaea for his education and persecuting activity, he has to move him back toward Damascus, where Paul says that Jesus appeared to him. That is how we get a photism "on the road to Damascus." Paul does not get to his destination under his own power—he has to be led into the town by companions ministering to his blind state.

Luke tells a great story, and it has entered the world's imagination. We hear all the time of "road to Damascus" experiences. This is the most famous conversion story in Christian history, rivaled only by Augustine's conversion in the garden, when he, too, receives an audition telling him to pick up a book and read. Both these stories are used as paradigmatic of conversion in classic accounts of the subject like William James's *The Varieties of Religious Experience* or Arthur Darby Nock's *Conversion*. This is unfortunate, since the event is not really a conversion, as even Luke will emphasize in his second and third tellings of it. But what is important here is to see how far the whole thing is from Paul's description of his dealings with Jesus. Paul tells us nothing of falling to the ground, being blinded, needing an Ananias to restore his sight—any more than we hear of such dramatic things happening when the risen Jesus appeared to Peter or James or the other followers. Luke's fiction has replaced far more interesting fact. Here as elsewhere we must look intently at Paul's own words to see what he actually meant. Luke will prove a continuing obstacle to this effort.

NOTES

1. A. M. Hunter argues that this part of Paul's letter is just what he declares at the outset, a credal formula he took from the tradition and is handing on. The wording, the prominence of the Jerusalem leader

James, the Aramaic form *Kephas,* Hunter argues, point to an origin in the Jerusalem church. *Paul and His Predecessors* (SCM Press, 1961), pp. 15–18, 117–18.

2. Mt 28.9–10, 17–19, Mk 16.12–18, Lk 24.13–49, Jn 20.14–18, 19–23, 26–29, 21.4–23.

3. A simpleminded objection to Paul's account of Jesus' apparition was that he would not have known how to recognize that it was actually Jesus, since he never saw him before the crucifixion. According to the Gospel accounts, even those who had lived with him had no advantage here. The risen body is a mystery not so easily explained; but Jesus surely knew how to make himself known.

4. For the importance of translating *Khristos* as "Messiah," see N. T. Wright, *The Resurrection of the Son of God* (Fortress Press, 2003), pp. 554–83.

5. The execution of Stephen, if it really occurred as Luke describes it, is explained as occurring during a "prefectural interstice," when Pontius Pilate was recalled to Rome in 36 CE and no replacement had taken office. See Raymond E. Brown, *The Death of the Messiah: From Gethsemane to the Grave* (Doubleday, 1993), p. 370. But Luke's whole treatment of Stephen is a theological construct in which the trial and execution are modeled closely on the trial and death of Jesus. Stephen too predicts the fall of the Temple, says that God is not confined to a single house of worship, is tried by Jewish authorities using false witnesses, says, "Receive my spirit," cries "with a loud voice," and prays, "Father, forgive them this sin" (Ac 6.13, 7.59–60). The whole scene is treated theologically, not historically.

2. Paul and the Pre-Resurrection Jesus

✝

GIVEN PAUL'S concentration on the risen Jesus he had encountered, some people take it for granted that he knew little about—or cared little to find out about—Jesus in the life he led before Paul was even aware of his existence. This view is strengthened by the assumption that Paul, a Jew of the Diaspora, seems not concerned with what occurred in Judaea. He emphasizes his distance from the Jewish center. This attitude apparently disturbed Luke, the author of the Acts of the Apostles, who tried to establish as many Pauline ties to Jerusalem as possible, bringing him there early to be trained by the great scholar Gamaliel. Some defenders of Luke have claimed that only in Jerusalem could Paul have acquired the knowledge he boasted of as a Pharisee, as one who outstripped his contemporaries in devout observance of the Law.

This argument underestimates the importance of the Diaspora in the first century of the Common Era. There were between 5 and 6 million Jews in the Diaspora, more than lived in Judaea. They made up more than 10 percent of most major cities in the Roman Empire—180,000 in Alexandria alone, and 50,000 in Rome.[1] The Greek word *diaspora* means "a scattering," and the Jews were scattered thick and wide. Though most Pharisees would no doubt have preferred to stay near the Temple and the full rites of their faith, scholarly men of the Law had reasons, like other influential Jews, to move around in the network of commercial, familial, and educational opportunities afforded by the rich Diaspora culture. We are told in the Gospel of Matthew (23.15) that the Pharisees were active missionaries. At a time of brisk travel, when there was intense traffic to and from Judaea, there is no reason Paul could not have had a full Pharisaical training in Tarsus, or later in Damascus, his two homes, neither of them far from Judaea, and both of them centers of trade and communication.

If Pharisaism was widespread in the Diaspora, so—almost overnight—was the Jesus movement widespread in Syria and Cilicia. There were already Brothers in Damascus and Antioch soon after Jesus' death—otherwise, how could Paul have persecuted them in the one place, and joined them in the other? And how, precisely, did he try to "extirpate" them (Gal 1.13)? Not, as Luke claimed, by arresting them and putting them to death. What instruments were available to him as a Jew in the Roman province of Syria? Where, for that matter, did he encounter the early Brothers? The obvious place is the synagogue. The Brothers had not broken with the synagogue in the early days. As a strict observer of the Law, Paul would resent those claiming to have seen the risen Jesus. False Messiahs were a constant threat to the upholders of the established

Law and to good relations with the Roman rulers. The Brothers were not merely outside the authorized observances. They would upset the crucial population of "Godfearers," those sympathetic outsiders who attended synagogues in considerable numbers as potential converts. These people, we shall see, proved important for Paul's future ministry, but in his observant days he would have feared the effect of the Brothers on these "fellow travelers," who might be drawn away from their initial attraction to the Jewish faith.

How could Paul prevent this? Obviously, by using the weapons we shall see him employ against opponents in the letters that have come down to us—fierce argument, fine distinctions of scriptural interpretation, sardonic humor, and denunciation. He would refute the intruders, ridicule them, drive them out, deprive them of a base in Damascus. That would indeed be an "extirpation." We can easily imagine him doing this against the Brotherhood after we have seen him doing it within that company. Here is how Wayne Meeks describes Paul at work on those he opposes in the Corinthian gathering:

A wealth of rhetorical devices clothes this appeal: curses and threats on the one hand, reminders of blessings on the other, ironic rebukes, shaming and sarcasm. All are ways of suggesting to the addressees that they are in danger of committing irreparable folly and of recalling them to their earlier sound judgment.[2]

It is true that Jews had won the right in some cities to discipline their own members—that is how Paul later came to be flogged five times by Jews. But this was a community action, calling for community support, and Paul never says that anyone but himself was involved in his "persecuting" activities. He did not have the authority to flog, any more than to arrest or put to death. It is true that, once he became a Brother, he threatened to visit his fellows in Corinth with a club (1 Cor 4.21), but that was comic bluster—provoked by the people in Corinth who had called him weak. His real weapon was always language, and the community responded with an acknowledgment that he had wounded them with a letter (2 Cor 7.8).

If in Damascus Paul's major form of persecution was exposure of what he felt were false claims, then he had to study those claims well before he came to accept them. What was he objecting to in the Brothers' presence at the synagogue? Not—yet—the observance of kosher laws or the necessity of circumcision. Those points of difference were not at stake—he would raise them once he became a Brother himself. The first witnesses to Jesus were circumcised men, and observant. Their initial difference from other Jews was that they proclaimed the resurrection of a crucified man, the very thing Paul would later call "an affront *(skandalon)* to Jews" (1 Cor 1.23). In other words, what would become the center of his own faith, the risen Jesus, was the thing he felt at first he had to oppose and "extirpate." Jesus' appearance to him would be the supreme refutation of all his own refutations of the Brothers.

Once Paul joined the Brothers, he had many of his new fellows to tell him about Jesus' life. Those five hundred witnesses to the Resurrection were obviously a mobile bunch. Three members of his missionary teams—Barnabas, Silvanus, and Mark—had probably come from Jerusalem as part of the first spread of the faith from the original followers.[3] Some who had joined the Holy before Paul did would cross and recross his path—the married team, for instance, of Prisca and Aquila he encountered and worked with in Corinth and Ephesus and Rome. By the time he wrote to Rome, where he had never been himself, Paul would greet over two dozen of the Holy who had gone there. Followers of Jesus were pullulating everywhere.

How did these active missionaries communicate the knowledge of their Lord? There were no Gospels yet. If any writings existed, they have perished, though they may have left traces in Paul's own letters and in later writings. Some hymns may have been written down. But we are dealing with a predominantly *oral* culture, one in which transmission viva voce was highly developed, along with the mnemonic skills such a culture entails. Jesus had spoken to many crowds, on many occasions. He had answered many questions, retold many parables. There was a rich store of memories from different people who had seen him in different contexts. The variations of what seem the same events or sayings in the Gospels are probably a thin harvesting of a wide variety of accounts originally circulated.

Paul did not have to go to Jerusalem to hear such accounts—though he could have confirmed many things when he met Peter and the others there. For that matter, he did not have to go to Jerusalem to talk with Peter. They would be active together in the gatherings at Antioch, and Peter's associates (if not Peter himself) were influential in Corinth. The Lord's brothers, too, were out traveling with their wives (1 Cor 9.5). Paul had frequent occasion to talk with people who had known Jesus in his lifetime, some whose names we know, many whose names we do not—and he had even more opportunities to talk with followers of those first associates who had committed oral traditions to their minds and hearts. He lived during his first days as a Brother in the gatherings of Damascus and Antioch, where he learned the rituals and traditions of his new faith. He had to learn before he could teach, and close study of his work shows that he did just that.[4]

But if Paul knew a great deal about the life of Jesus, why does he recount so little from it in his letters? There are several reasons for this. The letters are not expositions of the meaning of Jesus' life—though Paul could have engaged in that when he was with the gatherings he helped form. The letters are addressed to specific problems, and he uses material from Jesus' life only when that is needed for addressing those problems. When such citation of Jesus' words is called for, he has the right words at his command—on the Lord's Meal *(Kyriakon Deipnon)*, for instance, or on a case of divorce in the gathering, or on observance of kosher, or on the acceptance of financial support by an emissary. It has been argued that in these direct citations Paul's versions are probably closer to what Jesus said than are later records of it in the Gospels.

On the Lord's Meal, for instance, his report is not only the first—written decades before any of the Gospel versions—but probably the closest to what Jesus actually said. We should not fall into the fallacy of thinking that a saying of Jesus in one of the Gospels is "the original," which Paul only approximates in what seems to be a paraphrase of it. The truth could be the other way around. Out of the rich store of oral accounts that would be reflected in the Gospels, that which Paul received may be closer to Jesus' own words than are the variants in the Gospels.

Of the many places where Paul echoes the teaching of Jesus, consider just some:

1. When the Brothers in Rome differed over observance of kosher, Paul used the authority of Jesus to compose their differences: "I know, *relying on Lord Jesus*, that nothing is unclean of itself. Only if a man supposes it unclean does it become unclean for him" (Rom 14.14). Is that

Paul's fumbling toward what Jesus says in the Gospel of Matthew, answering those who accused him of flouting the purity code? "Understand what you hear from me: What a man takes into his mouth does not make him unclean. What comes out of his mouth—that is what makes him unclean" (Mt 15.10–11). Jesus in the Gospels frequently says that purity is a matter of the heart and intention, not of ritual observance: "Make sure your heart is not a darkness. If your whole body is suffused with light, no part of it is left in darkness, it will be light-giving, as when a lamp lights you with its brightness" (Lk 11.35–36). Paul gives us our first version of this teaching. He is not, necessarily, parroting what would not be written for years to come.

2. When the Brothers in Corinth made the meal of love an occasion for conflict, Paul reminded them of the instruction he had given them earlier on what Jesus said at that meal:

> What I received from the Lord I passed on to you— that the Lord Jesus, on the night he was betrayed, took bread and, after blessing it, broke it and said: "This is my body, which is for you. Do the same to keep the memory of me." Just so with a cup, after finishing dinner: "This cup is the new bond, in my blood. Do the same, as you drink it, to keep my memory." For as many times as you eat this bread

or drink this cup, you announce the death of the Lord, before his return. (1 Cor 11.23–26)

How did Paul learn this "from the Lord"? In a vision? He does not say that. He uses the language of tradition—what was handed to me I handed on—the same formula he had used for the basic creed he recites at 1 Corinthians 15.3. Where did he learn the tradition of the Lord's Meal? Obviously in the first gatherings where he took part in the Lord's Meal, in Damascus, in Antioch, where followers from Jerusalem had brought the revelation before Paul joined them. Those gatherings were as close as we can get to the actual night being commemorated. Paul is closer to that night than any of the three Gospels that quote Jesus' words. The Gospels, for that matter, differ from each other in the details of what was said, as well as from Paul's account— but his stands first in the tradition, and nearest to the source.

3. At Corinth, Paul actually got himself into trouble by quoting the words of Jesus. He had refused to let the Brothers there support him, but when the Corinthians learned that he had taken contributions from the gatherings in Macedonia, he had to admit: "The Lord directed that those who reveal the revelation should be supported *(zēn)* by revealing it" (1 Cor 9.14). He is referring to

directions Jesus gave when he first sent off any emissaries of the revelation. Jesus told them to take nothing
with them, not even a pouch to provide for future supply, but to eat what was offered where they were welcomed, since "he who does a work deserves support
(trophē) for it," as Matthew puts it (10.10). Or "deserves
payment" *(misthos)* for it, according to Luke (10.7).

Paul could not use, because he clearly did not know,
Luke's modification of the Lord's instruction. Jesus originally sent the emissaries out on a short errand to
nearby villages in Judaea. Missionary efforts of a long-
term and long-distance nature in urban areas made Luke
present Jesus as saying (22.36) that they could take provisions on later journeys. Paul has to justify himself in
another way, and it would be undiplomatic to give his
real reason for not taking support in Corinth. That city
was split venomously between a wealthier and a poorer
faction. The gulf even made their dinner of unity a
source of division, as the better-off ate and drank more
lavishly than the poorer Brothers (1 Cor 11.21–22). If
Paul, who wants to be the neutral reconciler, took support, it would obviously come from the wealthier Brothers, whom he is trying to correct. But to say this would
itself cause enmity. Instead, he says that the Lord's directive gave a right *(exousia,* 9.15) to the emissary that Paul
would rather not exercise. He even uses a play on words

to make his argument. He says that carrying the revelation is itself a reward *(misthos)* for him (9.17)—so this laborer has, as directed, received his pay! What is interesting for our purposes here is that Paul knows the Lord's directive and has to acknowledge it, even as he explains his departure from it.

4. The Corinthians had an endless supply of troubles to lay before Paul. One involved a divorce in the gathering. Once again Paul begins from the words of Jesus: "To the married I pronounce—no, it is not I, but the Lord—that a wife should not be separated from her husband; or if she does separate, she must either stay single or rejoin her husband; and a husband should not divorce his wife" (1 Cor 7.10–11). Paul refers to Jesus' teaching "What God has joined, let man not sunder" (Mk 10.9, Mt 19.6). When he allows for an exception, in the case of a Brother or Sister married to an unbeliever (1 Cor 7.12), he is careful to preface his remark: "It is I saying this, not the Lord" (7.12). In the same way, when he recommends celibacy, he says that this is his position, not one he has from the Lord (1 Cor 7.6–7, 25–26, 35, 40). His care to stay with the sayings of the Lord shows that he clearly knows them, far more of them than he needs to cite for meeting special problems.

5. Another teaching Paul says he has "from the Lord" concerns the end time. Like Jesus, Paul taught that Jesus had

fulfilled the Messianic prophecies by his coming, but that the completion of his mission was still to take place. But the Thessalonians feared that their Brothers who had died would not be part of that glorious consummation. To reassure them he writes:

> For this we tell you from the Lord's word: we who remain alive shall not go in before the dead when the Lord appears. Rather, at the summons, as the archangel cries out and God's trumpet sounds, the Lord will come down from heaven, and those who died in Messiah will rise up first, then we who remain living will be swept up with them in the clouds to meet the Lord aloft. After, we shall be with him forever. Give each other comfort with these words. (1 Thess 4.15–18)

Paul has a tradition from Jesus like that caught in the Gospel of Matthew:

> Then will appear in heaven a presage of the Son of Man, and all the tribes of the earth will lament, and they will see the Son of Man arriving on heaven's clouds in power and great splendor, and he will dispatch his angels with great trumpet flourishes, and they shall gather in his chosen ones from the four

winds, from one end of the heavens to the other. (Mt 24.30–31)

Like Jesus, Paul says that the consummation will come unexpectedly—"in an eyeblink" (1 Cor 15.52)—and the Brothers must be alert. It will come "like a thief in the night" (1 Thess 5.2)—a direct parallel with Matthew 24.43 and Luke 12.39–40. Is the report in Matthew any more authoritative than the far earlier one in Paul?

6. One saying of Jesus was particularly useful to Paul in his conflict with the "wise" ones of Corinth. In two of the Gospels, Jesus says, "I thank you, Father, Lord of heaven and earth, for hiding these things from the learned and the wise and revealing them to simple people" (Mt 11.25, Lk 10.21). Paul brought the saying to bear on his argument with the learned Corinthian faction: "God's ignorance surpasses human learning, and the trivial things of God surpass human importance. . . . We speak of the learning of God, kept as a secret hidden away, as he arranged ahead of time for our glory, a secret this time's important ones never penetrated" (1 Cor 1.25, 2.7–8).

7. Paul also echoes the claim of Jesus that the Temple is to be replaced by his body, and by the Brothers incorporated into that body, since the Spirit has his abode (*oikei*)

in them. The Spirit is no longer confined to one physical space. "Surely you must know that you are the Temple of God, and the Spirit of the Lord has his abode *(oikei)* in you. If anyone destroys the Temple of God, God will destroy him, for the Temple is holy, and you are it" (1 Cor 3.16–17; cf. 6.19, 2 Cor 6.16). "In Christ we became one body by baptism through the action of a single Spirit" (1 Cor 12.13). These passages are crucial, since it is often said that Jesus' claim in the Gospels that he is the Temple, replacing the old meeting place between God and man, is an invention that grew up only after the actual destruction of the Temple in 70 CE. But here is Paul saying the same thing almost two decades before the destruction of the physical Temple in Jerusalem. He is in perfect accord with the sayings of Jesus, and proves that this tradition was in circulation among the Brothers well before the Temple was destroyed—and even more clearly before the Gospels were written.

In the Gospels, when Jesus is rebuked for letting his followers violate the Sabbath, he responds: "In truth I tell that here you have something greater than the Temple" (Mt 12.6). When some scoff at his saying, "Destroy this Temple and in three days I will raise it again," the Gospel of John explains: "The Temple he referred to was his body" (Jn 2.19, 21). Jesus tells the Samaritan woman: "Believe me, the moment is coming when you will worship the Father neither on this mount [at the Samaritan Temple on Mount Gerizim] nor in Jerusalem. . . . The moment is coming, and is now here, when true worshipers will worship the Father in Spirit and in Truth" (Jn 4.21, 23). She says that this can occur only with the arrival of the Messiah—Paul's title for Jesus. Jesus responds to her, "I am he, I who tell you this" (4.26). Some might say John takes this from Paul, reversing what used to be said, that Paul draws on (and distorts) the Gospel. In any event, Paul is not saying things alien to what Jesus says in the later Gospels.

8. The belief that all the Brothers are members of Christ leads to the corollary that they are members of each other. "As we have in our body many members, and all the members do not perform the same function, so we, though many, are one body in Messiah, and serve as members of each other" (Rom 12.4–5). Jesus, after saying that "I am the vine, you the branches" (Jn 15.5), draws the corollary, "Love one another as I have loved you" (Jn 15.12). "I am in the Father, and you are in me, and I in you" (Jn 14.20). One Spirit pervades the vine and the body. This is the deeper meaning of the "Golden Rule" (Mt 7.12, Lk 6.31)—not simply that you should treat others as you would be treated, but treat them as if they were you (because *they are*).

9. Paul says that the essence of the Law is love, and Jesus

said the same. Here is Paul: "The entire Law is fulfilled in this one saying, Love your neighbor as yourself" (Gal 5.14). "The one who loves his neighbor has fulfilled the Law, since Commit no adultery, Steal not, Covet not—any commandment whatever—all are comprehended in this language: You shall love your neighbor as yourself. Love your neighbor and you can do no wrong. For love is what fulfills the Law" (Rom 13.8–10). And here is Jesus: "What you would have others do to you, do to them. That is the Law and the prophets" (Mt 7.12). "You shall love the Lord your God with your entire heart, your entire soul, your entire mind—that is the greatest and the first commandment. The second is its like: You will love your neighbor as yourself. From those two commands is the entirety of the Law derived" (Mt. 22.37–40).

This is the real point. Those who say that Paul's was an alien spirit superimposed on that of a loving Jesus do not see that they both taught the same message of love. Jesus told his followers to love their enemies (Mt 5.44, Lk 6.28). So did Paul: "If your enemy is hungry, give him to eat; if thirsty, give him to drink" (Rom 12.20). Jesus said, "Judge not, lest you be judged" (Lk 6.37), since only the sinless can judge others (Jn 8.7), and Paul said: "In convicting others you condemn yourself, since you are guilty of what you condemn" (Rom 2.1). And: "Who are you to be your brother's judge?" (Rom 14.10). Paul, like Jesus (Mt 7.1–2), said, "Take no revenge" (Rom 12.19). Jesus said not to resist one who wrongs you (Lk 6.28–30), and Paul directed others to submit to wrong rather than take people to court (1 Cor 6.7). In the Gospels, Jesus says, "Rescue comes from the Jews" (Jn 4.22), and Paul: "From Zion is the Rescuer" (Rom 11.26), and, "The revelation is God's miracle of rescue for one who believes—the Jew first, then the Greek" (Rom 1.16).

I am not saying that Paul had specific words of Jesus in mind for all these similarities. But he surely had grasped the key to what Jesus taught during his life on earth. Most would agree that the point of the Sermon on the Mount, of the Golden Rule, of the frequent commands to love unstintingly was deeply understood by a man who could write this:

Were I to speak the languages of all men and all angels, without having love, I were as a resonating gong or jangling cymbal. Were I to prophesy and know all secrets and every truth, were I to have faith strong enough to move mountains, without having love, I were as nothing. Were I to give away all my possessions, or give my body to be burned, without having love, it would avail me nothing.

Love is patient, is kind. It does not envy others or brag of itself. It is not swollen with self. It is not wayward or grasping. It does not flare with anger, nor harbor a grudge. It takes no joy in evil, but delights in truth. It keeps all confidences, all trust, all hope, all endurance. Love will never go out of existence. Prophecy will fail in time, languages too, and knowledge as well. For we know things only partially, or prophesy partially, and when the totality is known, the parts will vanish. It is like what I spoke as a child, knew as a child, thought as a child, argued as a child—which, now I am grown up, I put aside. In the same way we see things in a murky reflection now, but shall see them full face when what I have known in part I know fully, just as I am known. For the present, then, three things matter—believing, hoping, and loving. But supreme is loving. (1 Cor 13.1–13)

Does that sound like a man with what Nietzsche called "a genius for hatred"?

NOTES

1. Wayne Meeks, *The First Urban Christians: The Social World of the Apostle Paul,* second edition (Yale University Press, 2003), p. 34.

2. Ibid., p. 116.

3. Ibid., pp. 57, 60, 61.

4. Traces of prior Diaspora teachings are discovered in Paul by, among others, A. M. Hunter, *Paul and His Predecessors,* second edition (SMC Press, 1961), and David L. Dungan, *The Sayings of Jesus in the Churches of Paul* (Fortress Press, 1971).

3. Paul "on the Road"

☩

PAUL WAS, by any measure, a heroic traveler. It is estimated that he covered at least ten thousand miles, much of it on foot. He lived in a new age of travel, thanks to Roman roads-and-bridges engineering, as well as administrative military skills in the Pax Romana. Not that travel is ever entirely easy or safe. Brigands by land, pirates by sea, haughty officials, punishing weather, random chance, and dogging malice can never be eliminated—certainly not when one is on the road as much, and with as few resources, as Paul was. It has been said that Luke's Acts of the Apostles resembles a Hellenistic novel in its wonders and perils and hairbreadth escapes. Paul's own sober account is fairly hair-raising on its own:

> I have been more than they—more overworked, excessively beaten, more imprisoned, closer to death. Five times I was given forty-less-one lashes by the Jews, thrice clubbed, once stoned, thrice shipwrecked, a day and a night I spent in the sea—with many trudgings of the road, with river dangers, dangers from brigands, dangers from my people, dangers from outsiders, dangers by

town, dangers by country, dangers at sea, dangers from
pseudo-Brothers, with toil and effort, often sleepless,
with hunger and thirst, often without food, in cold, with
no covering. (2 Cor 11.23–27)

That would be a heroic catalogue for the most robust of
travelers. But Paul was, at least intermittently, sickly. He was
laid up, the first time he went to Galatia, by an illness that
could have tempted the Galatians to despise him (Gal
4.13–14): "You know that I brought you the revelation for the
first time because of a bodily debility, and in this test for you,
posed by my flesh, you showed no contempt or revulsion"
(this latter is a strong term—"you did not spew me out," *ex-
eptysate*). The passage is naturally read in conjunction with
Paul's statement that he had a "thorn in my flesh" to keep
him mindful of his weakness (2 Cor 12.7). Some plausibly argue that he was an epileptic. This is a recurring debility that
can be ridiculed, as we see from the case of Julius Caesar. At
any rate it was something he had to acknowledge, and which
he praised others for accepting. On the other hand, it may
help explain the attitude of the Corinthians who said that "his
letters are impressive and strong, but in person he is physi-
cally feeble and his speech contemptible" (2 Cor 10.10). His
physical debility, whatever it was, makes the catalogue of his
travels become all the more heroic—as does the manual labor

he performed despite this handicap. Obviously, a strong will drove a flagging body forward.

Compelling as these arduous travels are, they can be misleading. They can suggest Paul was always on the road, communicating only by letter with the Brothers he worked with and for. Actually, of course, his seven letters are exceptions to his normal way of speaking with the Brothers. He spent long and patient months with each community we know of. He began in the already established gatherings at Damascus and Antioch, and may have spent years there, where he was baptized, learning baptismal formularies and hymns echoed in his letters.[1] He often stayed in one place until driven out by Jews or Romans who considered him a troublemaker. Sometimes he left one or more of his coworkers with a community when he moved on, or sent back others to continue his activity. He maintained contact across the network of gatherings through traveling Brothers who went from one place to another on business or family errands or in special delegations to call for or supply help.

Luke has contributed to the hit-and-run atmosphere about some accounts of Paul's missionary activity. He gives the impression, for instance, that Paul stayed in Thessalonica for little more than three weeks before he had to flee persecution stirred up by Jews (Ac 17.1–10). But the Anchor Bible editor of the Letters to the Thessalonians, Abraham Malherbe, points out that Paul says he more than once received financial aid in Thessalonica sent from Philippi (Phil 4.16). Since arrangements and delivery for such aid would take weeks, if not months, he obviously spent considerable time establishing this first gathering in Greece. He refers to the manual labor he and his fellows engaged in, to support themselves while growing close to the community. He speaks in the plural, since the letter comes from Silvanus and Timothy as well as Paul:

> Our deep fondness for you made us ready to share with you not only the revelation of God but own our lives, so dear had you become to us. You remember, Brothers, our burdensome toil, working day and night so as not to impose on you while we expounded to you the revelation of God. (1 Thess 2.8–9)

That does not describe a brief visit but an intense commitment to the gathering.

Nonetheless, he was driven out by Jewish hostility (2.14). Though he was eager to see the Thessalonians again, his return was delayed, so he sent Timothy back to give his support to the young community (3.1–2). Far from being hit-and-run, his relations with the various gatherings were so close that he uses the most intimate terms to describe those relations. He feels always like the Brother he calls them, but also as tender as a nurse toward them (1 Thess 2.7), or a father (1 Thess 2.11), or a mother who has begotten them in pain (Gal 4.19). His message was one of love, which he had to practice as well as recommend. Even when he clashed with other Brothers, there is evidence he was reconciled with them—surely with Barnabas, and Apollos, and very probably with Peter. We see him angry in the letters, probably more often than people saw him showing wrath in their presence (2 Cor 10.9). Indeed, some Corinthians found him fiercer in letters, milder in person—though he tries to assure them that, in this case, it will be the opposite, that he will come in wrath if he has to come to them (1 Cor 4.21). But this storm, too, blows over.

What was he like for those who met him? Certainly he was persuasive, or he could not have won over so many people to new or enlarged gatherings. Though few people, on the evidence of the letters, would compare this fierce rhetorician with a Francis of Assisi, he must have had the kind of incandescent goodwill that makes loving ascetics so attractive. He took up menial labor among his fellows, asked for little, collected for the needs of others. Since he says he supported himself in Thessalonica, the aid he received from Philippi must have gone to help the poorer people he was calling into Brotherhood.

Tents?

WHAT KIND OF WORK did Paul labor at? It is interesting that he never tells us, only that it was hard and time-consuming ("night and day"). Luke says in the Acts that he was a tent maker, and this has generally been accepted. Some were disturbed that he would work in leather goods, which Jews did not consider quite clean. Even if he did not use pigskin, there was something contaminating to Jews about handling dead animals. Others contend that he could have worked in linen, since awnings and other shields from the sun were in great demand. Even that would have involved heavy sewing. Indeed, when Paul adds a postscript to one of his letters (which were all dictated to scribes), he draws attention to the large size of his writing (Gal 6.11). The Dominican scholar Jerome Murphy-O'Connor thinks this may be a reference to his gnarled fingers, toughened by drawing thread through heavy linen. Murphy-O'Connor believes that he was an artisan who carried his tool kit with him—though he acknowledges that Paul does not refer to his work in terms that reflect an artisan's pride. He calls it "burdensome toil" (1 Thess 2.9), and says, "We weary ourselves in hard labor with our hands" (1 Cor 4.12).

The belief in Paul's tent-making has led people to exercise their creative imaginations. Some suppose that Paul's father in Tarsus owned a tent-making business and Paul grew up knowing the trade. Luke more positively connects Paul's work with the tent-making business of his coworkers Prisca and Aquila (Ac 18.3). Luke seems to have good information about Prisca and Aquila, who were part of the Brotherhood before Paul was, and who traveled and knew many of the Brothers. So it is probably true that when Paul was with them he worked in their shop, along with other members of their firm, including slaves. In that case, Paul was probably speaking more than figuratively when he said, "I have made myself everyone's slave" (1 Cor 9.19).

But can we say, as many do, that tent making was Paul's trade everywhere he went? Remember that he and Silvanus and Timothy were working night and day in Thessalonica. Were they all tent makers? Could they expect to find enough tent-connected contracts for all of them wherever they went? Since Paul made much of his own labor and commended it to others, it is unlikely that his coworkers would have shirked toil. It seems far more likely that Paul and his fellows took up whatever jobs they could get in each community, however menial. For one thing, this would give them a place in the community while they made their initial contacts and began their instruction of people they found there.

If the members of the team could find work only in different shops or work yards, so much the better—they would have multiple points of engagement with others. Wayne Meeks makes the case that Paul's communities, though they covered a broad social span (omitting only the very top and the very bottom of society), had a core of mainly artisans and small-scale merchants. Working and teaching among them was Paul's way of becoming a Brother in fact as well as in profession. He boasts of his adaptability (1 Cor 9.19–22), and a willingness to take on even "slavish" tasks was one way of disarming new acquaintances.

With the Gatherings

HOW DID HE BEGIN in any town? Since every urban center in the Empire had a sizable Jewish quarter, that was the first place where he would have had some ties and recommendations. Luke says that he normally began by arguing in the synagogue, and only when driven out did he turn to the non-Jews (Ac 9.20). Some think that beginning in synagogues would compromise Paul's vocation to the uncircumcised. Both positions are no doubt too schematic. Paul preaches the Messiah as a reconciler of all Brothers. And both positions ignore the great middle area that was Paul's obvious hunting ground—the "Reverent People" *(Sebomenoi)*, also called "God-Revering" *(Theosebeis)*. These are normally referred to in English as "Godfearers" because of the form Luke uses at Acts 10.2 and 13.26, *Phoboumenoi ton Theon.*

The people thus variously referred to were inquiring and sympathetic non-Jews welcomed in synagogues, where they could study, pray, and contribute money or advice, without being (yet) circumcised. They might go on to full membership in the faith, or they might just help create goodwill for the Jews in their dealings with the "pagan" world. The Romans of the first century were out on quest for spiritual knowledge, and they welcomed many Eastern sects or cults—principally that of Mithras. But among the exotic beliefs being entertained, the Jews had, for some, a special appeal, based on their monotheism (in a polytheistic world), their purity of life, and their ancient learning. They were feared by some Romans precisely because they could attract curious and searching spirits, drawing people away from the imperial cult. Juvenal the satirist (14.96–106) attacked a father who observed the Sabbath and let his son be circumcised. For the poet, such men undermined the ancient Roman ways.

There were more Reverent People than used to be supposed. A synagogue inscription from the Roman city of Aphrodisias in Asia Minor shows that 43 percent of the donors, along with nine members of the governing board, were *Theosebeis*. Admittedly, the inscription comes from c 200 CE, but it reflects a long-standing trend in the culture. There was anti-Semitism in the Roman world, as Juvenal's poem shows, but Louis Feldman collected an astonishing number of favorable or admiring references to Jews in the ancient literature.[2] They give force to a comment by Robert Tannenbaum, a historian studying Aphrodisias:

Judaism, by the early third century, may well have been a more popular religion among the pagans, and therefore a more powerful rival to Christianity in the race for the soul of the Roman world, than we have had any reason to think until now. This helps us to understand the tension between the Church and the Synagogue in the first few centuries A.D.[3]

If Paul based his own mission on appeals to this body of Gentiles, his constant use of Jewish scripture in addressing them makes sense. They were interested in Moses before he offered them Jesus. This also helps explain Jewish hostility to Paul—he was drawing away people important to their own position in the Empire. Gerd Theissen, an expert on the sociology of Paul's world, is emphatic on this point:

God-fearers had already demonstrated an independence with reference to their native traditions and religion. They stood between differing cultural realms and were thus particularly receptive to the Christian faith, which crossed ethnic and cultural boundaries and offered an identity independent of inherited traditions. Judaism could not do this; within it these people would not be fully entitled. Christianity, however, especially in its Pauline form, offered them the possibility of acknowledging monotheism and high moral principles and at the same time attaining full religious equality without circumcision, without ritual demands, without restraints which could negatively affect their social status. Seen in this light, the conflict between Christianity and Judaism is easier to understand: the Christian mission was luring away the very Gentiles who were Judaism's patrons. . . . Not only did their contributions now benefit the Christian community, but the Jews, as a minority, had come to depend on the recognition and advocacy of such people in a foreign Gentile world full of anti-Jewish prejudices.[4]

There is no reason to think Paul worked exclusively with *Theosebeis*. But they would have given him a base originating in the synagogue, from which he could move out into their own broader network of relatives, friends, and associates. When he said he made himself all things to all people—a Jew with Jews, a Gentile with Gentiles—he was speaking of this intermediate area where he could move about bringing religion to those who were already drawn to it.

How did Paul address these people in their intimate gatherings (and not by long-range emergency missives)? It is clear that he brought them the revelation—that is, the fulfillment of the Messianic hopes in the death and Resurrection of Jesus. For expounding the Messianic tradition he was well equipped by his Pharisaic training. When he needs a clinching passage from scripture, he has it at hand, no matter where he is, on the road or away from libraries. Which raises the question of his education. Did he study with Gamaliel after all? Not unless he was lying when he said he was unknown in Judaea. There was learning in the Diaspora. But how had Paul afforded it? Was his father a rich tent maker? We simply do not know. However he managed it, he clearly got a good education—though he quotes Jewish scripture in the Septuagint Greek, not the Hebrew. That could, of course, be because he is addressing Greek speakers. But scholars find even his interpretation of passages relying more on the Septuagint than the Hebrew—another point against his having studied with Gamaliel.

What of Paul's broader education in the Greek culture of the Diaspora? Here scholars have swung from one extreme to the other over the years. When it was thought that Paul was jettisoning Jewish wisdom for Greek philosophy, many credited him with more Hellenic influence than can be sustained by careful study of his works. He never quotes a Greek or Roman philosopher. The pendulum swung decisively against the Hellenistic thesis in the influential work of E. P. Sanders, who renewed the thesis of Albert Schweitzer that Paul was a Jewish apocalyptic teacher. But this view has been tempered recently by intense work on the rhetoric of Paul, which shows a familiarity with Greek arguing styles, epistolary, didactic, and celebratory ("epideictic"). He is especially good at the competitive didactics of the Stoic "diatribe" (literally, "a wearing down"). Cynics like Epictetus taught in short bursts of simulated debate, with imagined interrogators challenging the master. This can produce a kind of instructive self-heckling. Here is Paul on the defensive:

> Has circumcision any use at all?
>   Yes, in every respect . . .
>
> If Jews broke trust with God, does that make God abandon trust?
>   Far from it . . .
>
> Is it wrong of God to be angry (to put it in human terms)?
>   Far from it . . .
>
> Are we Jews then superior?
>   Not in all ways . . .
>
> Do we cancel the Law with faith?
>   Far from it. We give the Law a firm basis . . .
>
> Is the Law itself sin?
>   Far from it . . .
>
> Was the Law, good in itself, deadly to me?
>   Far from it . . .
>
>   (Rom 3.1–5, 8, 31, 7.7, 13)

How he filled in the answers to this staccato drumbeat of questions shows the dialectical skills of Paul. The questions he here fires at himself are the kind he would have encouraged his interlocutors to direct at him in person. This method is the opposite of Socratic questioning. It is *being* questioned, an oral strategy echoed in his writing. It is easy to imagine members of his team supplying the questions if others were slow to raise them. Paul and his comrades proselytized together, as he reminds us in letters that say, "*We* brought you the revelation."

Paul's rhetorical skills are never clearer than when he abjures them. When the Corinthians decided that he was not as wise or eloquent as other "high-flying emissaries" who had come among them, he uses a kind of verbal judo, prevailing with a show of weakness. His critics boast of a superior wisdom and strength. He will boast of folly and feebleness:

Messiah did not make it my task to baptize you but to bring you the revelation, not in any learned words, lest the cross of the Messiah be a thing superfluous. What the cross says is to the abandoned sheer ignorance, but to those rescued it is God's miracle. For scripture says, "The learning of the learned I will obliterate, and the intelligence of the intelligent I will sweep aside." Where does that leave the learned of this age, where the scholar, where the quibbler? Has not God made the world's learning an ignorance? By the learning of God, the world's learning was useless for finding God. He chose to rescue those who trusted the ignorant revelation. So while Jews ask for miracles and Greeks seek learning, we reveal nothing but Messiah crucified—to Jews an affront, to Greeks ignorance, yet to us, the summoned, whether Jew or Greek, Messiah as God's miracle and God's learning. For God's ignorance surpasses human learning, and the trivial things of God surpass human importance.

Just think how you were summoned, Brothers—not many of you learned in human terms, not many important, not many highborn. But the ignorant things of this world God singled out to baffle the learned, and the trivial things of this world God singled out to baffle the important. The low and contemptible things God singled out, mere nothings, to baffle the somethings, so that what is human could show no pride before God. You, however, are now by his favor in Messiah-Jesus—who is our learning by God's favor, our vindication and hallowing and release, in accord with scripture: "Would you take pride, in the Lord take your pride."

For these reasons, Brothers, when I came to you I came with no pretentious speeches or teachings to announce what is established by God. I made up my mind not to display any learning to you, only Messiah, and him as crucified. For myself, I was weak and fearful and trembling before you, and my message for you, my preaching, was not persuasive by any eloquence, but in the mere presence of Spirit and miracle, so your faith would not rest on any human wisdom but only on God's miracle.

There is a kind of learning in our words, but only for

those who can take it in—not a learning of this age, or of those important in this age, who are perishing. We speak of the learning God kept as a secret hidden away, as he arranged ahead of time for our glory, a secret this time's important ones never penetrated—if they had, they would not have crucified the Lord of splendor. According to scripture: "What no eye saw, what no ear heard, what was never in the human heart—all that has God laid up for those who love him." This is what God has revealed to us by the Spirit. (1 Cor 1.17–2.10)

We should all have so little eloquence!

NOTES

1. Scholars have found traces of baptismal formulas or hymns at Rom 6.3–4, 1 Cor 6.11, 10.1–3, 12.13, Gal 3.27, Phil 2.6–11.

2. Louis Feldman, *Jew and Gentile in the Ancient World: Attitudes and Interaction from Alexander to Justinian* (Princeton University Press, 1993), p. 124.

3. Quoted in John Dominic Crossan and Jonathan L. Reed, *In Search of Paul: How Jesus' Apostle Opposed Rome's Empire with God's Kingdom* (HarperSanFrancisco, 2004), p. 27.

4. Gerd Theissen, *The Social Setting of Pauline Christianity: Essays on Corinth*, edited and translated by John H. Schultz (Fortress Press, 1982), pp. 103–4.

4. Paul and Peter

✝

PAUL REPEATEDLY makes it clear that he had the prickliest of relationships with the Brothers in Jerusalem. He went to that city only three times, each time with reluctance or trepidation. Luke, in the Acts of the Apostles, tries to obfuscate this matter. He has Paul making six trips there, counting an early one to study with Gamaliel. He takes him to the scene of Stephen's stoning, and gives him commissions from high priest and Sanhedrin to drag people from their homes and execute them. Then, after sending him with instructions from Jerusalem to Damascus, he presents his call from Jesus as occurring on the trip there. After this, he brings him back five times to what he takes to be the center of Christian life. The maps of Paul's travels—those polychrome spaghetti tangles in old Bibles—are based on Luke's exaggerated backings-and-forthings. No wonder the impression formed in some minds was of a man who never had time to stay with any gathering, so constantly was he on the move. Luke wants to present Paul as constantly "checking back with headquarters," as it were—though Paul emphatically denies that he ever did such a thing.

Luke is writing after the leader of the Brothers in

Jerusalem, James the brother of the Lord, has been killed—an event cited in Josephus's *Jewish Antiquities* (20.200). This took place after the break between James and the Jewish authorities in Jerusalem and before the destruction of the Temple by the Romans (in 70 CE). In Luke's time, therefore, the Jesus movement had been almost totally deracinated from its Jerusalem origins, and was being tugged in many directions. Luke tried to re-create a Jerusalem hub in his memory of the past, at a time when developments were shaking believers apart. He especially wanted to contain the Pauline mission within a central Jerusalem focus. He presents Paul's dealings with the founding generation in that city as an anachronistic Apostolic Council, in which Paul was given his mandate to the uncircumcised. He must reconcile that claim with Paul's own assertion that he was given his assignment directly from Jesus. One way Luke circumvents the difficulty is to let Peter pre-empt Paul's mission to the nations.

Peter's Vocation

THOUGH LUKE DEVOTES more of his narrative to Paul, since the Diaspora gatherings were the more successful ones, he gives Peter the leading role in almost every respect. The founding of the Christian church takes place, for Luke, in Jerusalem on the occasion of Pentecost, when Peter preaches the long first statement of the revelation to the nations.

Though the event takes place in Jerusalem, Peter is given a world audience, and his words go out in every possible language.

> We each hear it in our native tongue—Parthians and Medes and Elamites, and those who dwell in Mesopotamia, Judaea and Cappadocia, Pontus and Asia, Phrygia and Pamphylia, Egypt and the regions of Libya near Cyrene, Romans stationed here, Jews and proselytes, Cretans and Arabs, all of us hear them speaking in our own dialects of God's greatness. (Ac 2.8–11)

Paul says that at his confrontation with Peter and James in Jerusalem, he was given a mission to the nations and Peter to the circumcised; but Luke says that Peter was the first to be sent by God to the Gentiles. Peter leaves Jerusalem (where James the brother of the Lord is left as leader) to be an emissary to Lydda, Joppa, and Caesarea. As he came near Caesarea (the way Luke made Paul come near Damascus), Peter is given a vision that solved ahead of time Paul's problem of Gentiles forced to observe kosher laws.

> He was hungry and would eat. As others prepared a meal, he was rapt in a vision—he sees heaven open and some preparation like a great sheet lowered toward the earth by its four corners, and in it were all earth's quadrupeds and serpents, and air's flitting things. And a voice

sounded: "On your feet, Peter, to slaughter these and eat them." But Peter answered: "That is impossible, Lord, since I have never eaten profane and unclean things." And the voice came back: "Whatever God makes is clean, do not profane it." Three times this was repeated, then the preparation was snatched up to the sky. (Ac 10.10–16)

As it turns out, God has prepared a Reverent Person *(Theosebēs)* for Peter's arrival in Caesarea, and when Peter reaches his house he tells him: "You realize that the Law forbids a Jew's mixing with or entering the house of a Gentile. But God has shown me to call no one profane or unclean" (10.28). Luke has solved beforehand all the problems Paul later describes in his mission to the nations. Only then can Luke allow Paul to be called to that mission. Thus, after Peter has prepared the way, Paul can receive his (secondary) vocation to the nations.

Paul's Vocation

I HAVE ALREADY PRINTED the first of Luke's three accounts of Paul's call. The third one makes clear that this is a vocation story, based on the calls to ancient prophets, not a conversion story. Luke presents Paul as giving his own account—to King Agrippa during a hearing in Caesarea (exactly where Peter opened the mission to the Gentiles):

"At one time I considered it incumbent on me to do everything I could against the name of Jesus from Nazareth. I undertook this in Jerusalem, where I clapped many of the Holy into prison by mandate of the chief priests; and when their executions were decided, I voted for that. In every synagogue I tried to force them under torture to recant. My frenzy against them was so extreme that I hunted them down in foreign cities. One such was Damascus, where I was traveling with authority and warrants from the chief priests when at noon, Your Majesty, I saw a flash brighter than the sun lightning all about me and those journeying with me. As we all fell to the ground I heard a voice speaking to me in Aramaic: 'Saul, Saul, why are you persecuting me? It only hurts you to kick back when goaded.' But I said, 'Who are you, Lord?' And the Lord answered, 'I am Jesus, whom you are persecuting. But rise up and stand firm on your feet. This is why I have appeared to you, to single you out as my worker, as a witness to what you have seen of me and what further things I shall reveal to you, as I rescue you from your people and from the nations to which I am sending you, that you may open their eyes and turn from darkness to light, from Satan's thrall to God, so they may by faith in me gain forgiveness of sins and a share with the Holy.' " (Ac 26.9–18)

After the preliminary nonsense about Paul torturing people in every synagogue of Judaea and putting Brothers to death, Luke fashions Paul's vocation on that of Ezekiel—just as, in his Gospel, he took Jewish canticles and created the songs of Mary, Zachariah, and Simeon for his nativity stories. Ezekiel too is stunned by a bright light:

> When I saw that, I threw myself on my face and heard a voice speaking to me. "Man," he said, "stand up and let me talk with you." As he spoke a spirit came into me and stood me on my feet, and I listened to him speaking. He said to me, "Man, I am sending you to the Israelites, a nation of rebels who have rebelled against me. Past generations of them have been in revolt against me to this very day, and this generation to which I am sending you is stubborn and obstinate. When you say to them, 'These are the words of the Lord God,' they will know that they have a prophet among them, whether they listen or whether they refuse to listen because they are rebels. But you, man, must not be afraid of them or of what they say, though they are rebels against you and renegades, and you find yourself sitting on scorpions. There is nothing to fear in what they say, and nothing in their looks to horrify you, rebels though they are. You must speak my words to them, whether they listen or whether they refuse to listen, rebels that they are. But you, man, must listen to what I say and not be rebellious like them." (Ezek 1.28–2.8)

Luke's model, with assurances against the threats of the people among whom Ezekiel is being sent, explains the words he gives Paul about being "rescued from your people and from the nations." This fits Luke's scheme, in which Paul is threatened mainly by "his people"—namely the Jews. It does not fit so well with the threat Paul himself feels, as coming from his fellow Brothers. That problem comes to a head in Paul's description of his encounter with the Brothers in Jerusalem, seventeen years after his call to take the revelation to the nations. Luke's account of this meeting has been called, anachronistically, the Apostolic Council, even the First General Council of the church.

The Jerusalem Encounter

IN LUKE'S VERSION of this meeting, delegates from the Jerusalem gathering went to Antioch to demand that all Gentile Brothers be circumcised. After much debate over this, the Antiochenes commissioned Paul, Barnabas, "and some others" to defend their practice of noncircumcision before "the emissaries and elders" in Jerusalem (Ac 15.1–3). When this party presented its case to the gathering there, some Pharisaic Brothers repeated the demand for circumcision. Then the "emissaries and elders" went into formal session to decide the matter. "After an intense examination," Peter rose to speak. He referred people back to the vision in which he was ordered by heaven to eat "unclean" food, and said that this proved the old Law was no longer mandatory. One wonders why, given that preceding event, there was any doubt to be cleared up by the "council." As if to clinch the matter, James, the real authority in Jerusalem, then says: "Hear me, Brothers, Simeon gave an account of how God took steps to form from the nations a people in his name." Many commentators think James uses "Simeon" as a variant of Simon (Peter)—that is, he is telling them again what Peter just told them. It seems more likely that Luke is referring to his own poetic creation, the canticle of Simeon in his Gospel's nativity narrative. When Mary and Joseph take the child Jesus to the Temple, Simeon predicts that their baby is "a light to be unveiled to the nations" (Lk 2.32). The objection to this is that James's audience would not, presumably, have known what happened in Jesus' infancy. But neither, for that matter, would Luke have known. And if he can proclaim the event in his Gospel, why can he not refer to it in his Acts? It is not the least plausible of his inventions.

James then goes on to quote the prophet Amos as saying that God will gather in "all the nations among whom my name is invoked" (Ac 15.17). This says that Gentiles will be called, but it does not settle whether circumcision will be demanded of them. Nonetheless, James says that, given God's call to the Gentiles, the Brothers should not "heap up hindrances" to their responding. They should confine the rules for them to a few essentials—namely, that they refrain from pollution by idols, from sexual license, from animals that have been strangled, and from blood (Ac 15.19–20). Luke does not notice that these restrictions conflict with the vision of Peter, which said that *no* foods are unclean—including, presumably, blood and food from strangled animals. Nonetheless, the "emissaries and elders, along with the entire gathering," decided that these four demands should be promulgated.

This has been called "the Apostolic Decree," and Luke makes its enactment as formal as he can. After being written out, it is sent by way of two delegates from the Jerusalem gathering for delivery to Antioch. The delegates read it out before the assembled Antiochenes, who formally accept it and acclaim the delegates as prophets, and Luke seals the entire proceeding with an outpouring of the Spirit (Ac 15.22–33). This account is formal, hierarchical, legalistic, based on precedent. At every step of the process, forms are required and fulfilled. Luke is not only invoking the structures of his day but helping to advocate and create them.

Paul's account of the event—written, remember, three or more decades before Luke put down his version—could not be more different. There, Paul is neither summoned by Jerusalem nor sent by Antioch. He goes as a result of a vision urging him to go. He takes the uncircumcised Titus with him, to make him a test case. He does not submit his case to a formal meeting but to a private session with the so-called leaders. Peter's vision is not brought up—so the issue of kosher food (as opposed to circumcision) is not discussed. There is no formal decree sent by Jerusalem and accepted at Antioch, making four demands—there is a simple handshake extended by Peter and James. Paul is describing the charismatic conditions of the early gatherings, not the nascent church Luke would like to will into being.

Fourteen years passed before I went again to Jerusalem, this time with Barnabas, and taking along Titus as well. I went in response to a vision. I explained to them the revelation I reveal to the nations, but in private, with the apparent leaders, lest the course I was pursuing, or had pursued, should be discounted. But far from that: Titus, the Greek I brought with me, was not circumcised under compulsion, despite some interloping pseudo-Brothers, who slyly entered [Antioch] to spy on the freedom we were exercising in Messiah-Jesus, to return us to slavery—but to their dictates we gave not an instant's submission; rather, the real meaning of the revelation was maintained for you [Galatian Gentiles]. As for the apparent leaders, how important they were I care not (God does not play favorites), but they were the apparent ones, and they had no suggestions for me, but rather recognized that the revelation for the uncircumcised was entrusted to me, and that for the circumcised to Peter, since the same one who inspired Peter as an emissary to the circumcised had inspired me to go to the nations. Recognizing the divine favor granted me, James and Peter and John, the apparent pillars there, sealed things with a handshake, so we should serve the nations and they the circumcised, the only other point being that we keep in mind their needy ones, which I was eager to do. (Gal 2.1–10)

The Blowup at Antioch

PAUL AND LUKE agree that the question at Jerusalem was circumcision. Luke also says that modified kosher rules were upheld. But Paul's account of another event, his clash with Peter in Antioch, treats this as a matter far from settled. Luke has to omit this event entirely, since it contradicts two of his stories—that of Peter's vision and that of the Jerusalem conference where that vision was cited as a guide for others to follow. When Peter and Paul were both in Antioch, a warning came to Peter from James in Jerusalem, telling him he should not be eating nonkosher meals with the Gentile Brothers. Peter complied with this directive from James—which infuriated Paul, for whom the Lord's Meal was the symbol of unity for all the Brothers, Jew or Gentile. His anger is not disguised as he reports the disagreement with Peter. He is so mad that he makes up a brand-new contemptuous word—*ïoudaïzein*, which seems to mean not *being* a Jew but *playing at* being a Jew.

When Kephas came to Antioch, I rebuked him face-to-face, since he had no leg to stand on. Before the arrival of some men dispatched by James, he ate with those from the nations. But after they came, he withdrew from them into an isolation, intimidated as he was by the circumcisionists. The other Jews [Jewish Brothers] were just as hypocritical, and Barnabas was caught up in their hypocrisy. When I saw that they were not hewing to the clearly marked meaning of the revelation, I told Kephas before everyone, "If you, a Jew by birth, do not follow Jewish ways, how dare you make pretend-Jews of those from the nations?" (Gal 2.11–14)

It is easy to see why Luke could not tell this story. Some in later times would wish that Paul had not told it. Saint Jerome was so shocked by the idea that Peter and Paul could squabble that he claimed they did not really disagree but were putting on a kind of didactic charade. They had cooked up a way of dramatizing the truth that external rites are unimportant. Some people are still unable to face the fact that the great men could differ—Walther Schmithals, for instance, says that Paul just excoriates Peter as a cover for his own more important disagreement with Barnabas.[1] Even those who admit that Paul had reason to resent Peter's backpedaling on Jewish observance think he overreacted to mere eating arrangements. But for Paul it was not simply the unity of the Lord's Meal that was at stake. The risen Jesus was alive and present in Antioch in all those baptized into his mystical body. For Peter to withdraw from the presence of the risen Jesus was to repeat the rejection of Jesus. It was to throw up a barrier—pretend Jewishness—related to the barrier that had refused to extend the divine rescue to all nations. We learn from his reaction to faction in Corinth what he thought of dismembering the body of Christ.

Paul's Chronology

PAUL PUTS the blowup in Antioch after his account of the conference in Jerusalem, and most people treat the two events in that order, as I just have. But there is something suspect about this order. Why, if the handshake of peace had settled in principle the matter of enforcing the Law with Gentile Brothers, was it so quickly reopened? And why, if Barnabas was on Paul's side in Jerusalem, did he desert him on a similar issue in Antioch? And why does Paul later refer to Barnabas as if there had been no split between them (1 Cor 9.6)? Those who follow the account in Galatians seem to think that a parting of the ways took place between them after the Antioch dispute; but Luke says they argued over continuing to work with John Mark, who had left them in Pamphylia (Ac 15.36–39). That still does not explain Paul's later reference to Barnabas.

But there is reason to think Paul was not narrating chronologically in Galatians but arguing climactically—that he saved the conflict with Peter to show that he took a very firm stand on application of the Law, since that was the issue he was addressing among the Galatians. Since his argument there is over the kosher laws, it flows naturally out of the stand he took in Antioch. In fact, the argument comes so seamlessly out of the Antioch narrative that an editor of the letter says it is hard to say where the one ends and the other begins.

> Attempts to locate the end of the episode present a famous puzzle, sensed even by the earliest interpreters of the letter. In v. 14 Paul reports an incisive comment he made to Peter in front of the Antioch church, doing so with a clarity that enables one confidently to place the first of the quotation marks—"You, a Jew by birth, are living . . ." But he gives no clear indication as to where his remark to Peter ends, although by the time the reader comes to the final verses of chapter 2, he knows that he is no longer hearing the speech that Paul made to Peter in Antioch. Indeed, as regards literary form, the concluding verses of the chapter are unlike anything the reader of Galatians has encountered earlier. In fact, Paul's failure formally to close the quotation begun in v. 14 is no accident. It reflects his determination to connect his account of the Antioch incident to the situation in Galatia.[2]

In other words, the Antioch story *had* to come after the Jerusalem one to make possible this meld with the following argument.

Gerd Lüdemann argued for this order, noting that Paul does not introduce the Antioch event with his normal word for chronological sequence, *epeita*, "then . . ." (with the sense of "next"). Instead he says "but when . . ." *(hote de)*.[3] If we follow this sequence, then the clash over the food laws in Antioch caused a division that Paul, acting on a "revelation," took before the Brothers in Jerusalem. He and Barnabas go there, not as delegates from the Antioch gathering, as Luke would have it, but as people with a disagreement they meant to thrash out. It should be noted that Paul says he went there with Barnabas, but "*I* explained to them the revelation *I* reveal to the nations." Paul and Barnabas are not speaking together, as in Luke's picture of them as members of a delegation.

When the dispute is settled and the handshake of peace seals the agreement, then Paul's relations with Barnabas can continue amicably—and, for that matter, with Peter. Paul brings up the prior conflict only because the Galatians are acting as if the matter of food laws were *not* settled. This order makes better sense, as well as uncovering the sequence which Luke has re-created in his eirenic fashion. He talks of a problem in Antioch that is followed by a submission of the matter to Jerusalem for adjudication. The Antioch clash is thus referred to in the proper sequence, but in a disguised and ameliorative way.

If this is the sequence, then Paul's last reported dealings with Peter were not at the blowup in Antioch but after the handshake of peace in Jerusalem. This would accord with the tradition, well founded as I shall argue, that Peter continued to be an emissary in the Diaspora and ended with Paul in Rome, where they died together as victims of Nero's mad reaction to the fire that destroyed the city. The treatment of them as ultimately partners, seen in the early letters of Clement of Rome and Ignatius of Antioch, would thus be justified. The two great leaders ended up on the same side.

NOTES

1. Walther Schmithals, *Paul and James* (Alec R. Allenson, 1965), pp. 63–78.

2. J. Louis Martyn, *Galatians* (Doubleday, 1998), pp. 229–30.

3. Gerd Lüdemann, *Paul, Apostle to the Gentiles: Studies in Chronology,* translated by F. Stanley Jones (Fortress Press, 1984), pp. 75–77. With some hesitation, Rainer Riesner accepts Lüdemann's Antioch-Jerusalem sequence, in *Paul's Early Period: Chronology, Mission Strategy, Theology,* translated by Doug Stott (Eerdmans, 1998), pp. 232, 322.

5. Paul and Women

✝

PAUL BELIEVED in women's basic equality with men. He does not deserve the primary credit for this attitude. It was given to him in the practice of the Diaspora gatherings he first joined, as in the baptismal formula whose hymn form he records:

> Baptized into Messiah
> you are clothed in Messiah,
> so that there is no more
> Jew or Greek,
> slave or free,
> "man and woman,"
> but all are one,
> are the same in Messiah-Jesus.
>
> (Gal 3.26–28)

The hymn does not keep perfect symmetry by saying "man *or* woman," since this is a quotation from Genesis ("man *and* woman he created them," 1.27). There is no more "man and woman" as originally divided, since they are now united in Messiah—a concept Paul would expound when he said that the reborn Brother and Sister are "a new order of being" (*ktisis*, 2 Cor. 5.17).

The early gatherings of the Brothers were the most egalitarian groups of their day. Paul worked with, paid tribute to, and received protection from his Sisters in Messiah. There would be a concerted effort, over entire centuries, to hide or diminish this fact. There is no more spectacular instance of this than what was done to Junia, his fellow by background, his prison mate, his fellow emissary, and one who joined the Brotherhood before he did (Rom 16.7).

Junia

IN THE LONG list of people Paul greets at the end of his letter to the Romans, he gives special notice to the husband and wife evangelical team of Andronicus and Junia (Rom 16.6–7), whom he calls "my kindred" *(suggeneis mou)*. That could mean his fellow Jews—he used the term in that sense earlier in this letter (Rom 9.3)—though Wayne Meeks thinks it meant Paul's countrymen, from Cilicia or even from his hometown of Tarsus.[1] By stressing that he knows of their baptism before his—they were "reborn before me in Messiah"— Paul may be referring to the early days when he was meeting those already in the Diaspora gatherings where he was inducted, in Syria and Cilicia. At any rate, he feels a special bond with these two, since they have been his fellow prisoners *(synaichmalōtoi).* That word could mean that they were actually incarcerated with him (at Ephesus or Philippi) or simply that they too had been prisoners at some time. The former seems more likely here, since he is stressing their kindred closeness. The supreme accolade comes when he calls them "outstanding among the emissaries."

Though there are no offices in the early gatherings, only functions, and though Paul stresses the equal dignity of all gifts of the Spirit, he does list emissaries *(apostoloi)* first in the "big three" charisms—emissaries, prophets, and teachers (1 Cor 12.28). For Junia to be included not only among the emissaries but among the outstanding *(episēmoi)* ones was a high honor, as John Chrysostom recognized in his commentary on Romans: "How great this woman's love of wisdom *(philosophia)* must have been, to merit her inclusion among the apostles." She and her husband had a liturgy devoted to them as married saints and apostles in the Byzantine church. Most early commentators and fathers of the church, including Origen and Rufinus, celebrated her extraordinary eminence.

But sometime in the Middle Ages, apparently before the ninth century, it was decided that a woman apostle was unthinkable. This offended the male monopoly of church offices and honors that had grown up by that time, so Junia had to be erased from history. It took only a little smudging to do this. Paul uses her Greek name, *Iounia,* in the accusative case, *Iounian.* A mere change in accent markings (a circumflex over

the last vowel) would make it the accusative form of a hypothetical male name, *Iounias*. But there is one problem here.
"Junias" is *only* a hypothetical name—it never occurs in all
the ancient literature and inscriptions—whereas Iounia is a
common name, occurring hundreds of times. Besides, the
other teams Paul mentions in Romans 16 are male-female
ones—Aquila and Prisca, Philologus and Julia, Nereus and
Olympas—with the exception of a female-female one
(Tryphaena and Tryphosa, probably sister Sisters). We know
from Paul's reference to Peter and the Lord's brothers, who
traveled with their wives, that male-female evangelical teams
were common (1 Cor 9.5). Only the most Soviet-style rewrit-
ing of history could declare Junia a nonperson and invent a
new team, Andronicus and the philologically implausible Junias. Paul was generous to his female coworkers, a title he
proudly gave them.

Prisca

PAUL BEGINS his long list of those he greets in Rome with
Prisca and Aquila, another wife-husband team of Jews baptized before he was. He had met them after their earlier expulsion from Rome under Claudius (49 CE), evangelized with
them in Ephesus and Corinth, and worked in their tent-
making firm (Ac 18.3). While he was in Ephesus, he sent

greetings to Corinth from their house-gathering there (1 Cor 16.19). His present salute to them, at the top of his long list in Romans 16, suggests that he had sent them back to Rome to prepare for his visit there—though they have been there long enough to have a gathering in their home (16.5). Paul's knowledge that other acquaintances of his had reached Rome probably came from Prisca and Aquila, his primary correspondents, who also informed him of the local problems addressed in this letter, to a place he had not visited himself.

Prisca is usually listed first, before her husband, in Paul's letters and in the Acts of Luke (who seems to have had good sources on Prisca and Aquila). In the status-conscious Roman world, this prior listing meant higher dignity, on some ground or other. Meeks says that a freeborn woman would be listed before a freedman husband, or a noble one before a commoner.[2] Prisca might have been the wealthier holder in their tent-making firm—her dowry, for instance, could have included slaves to work the business. Some opine that she preceded her husband in baptism and helped instruct him, or took the lead in their evangelizing activities; Luke puts Barnabas before Paul in the early days of their evangelizing, which may indicate that Paul was the junior partner at that point (Ac 11.30, 12.25, 13.2). It has even been claimed that Prisca had a hand in the Pauline pseudepigrapha or in composing the Letter to the Hebrews. But the egalitarianism of the Brothers counts against thinking that she "outranked" her husband in theological terms. Probably it was a social convention of their past—in Pontus, according to Luke (Ac 18.2)—that gave her a priority.

Phoebe

PAUL SENDS his letter to the Romans by way of the woman he introduces in it, emphasizing her importance both to him and to the Brothers in general, so that she may get any cooperation she asks for in Rome. He has had an important history with her, as with Prisca and her husband.

> I commend to you our Sister, Phoebe, an attendant *(diakonos)* of the gathering in Cenchraeae, for welcome in the Lord as one of the Holy. Please support her in anything she may require, since she has been the protectress *(prostatēs)* of many others besides myself. (Rom 16.1–2)

Cenchraeae is the port of Corinth, so Phoebe had stood with Paul in his very troubled dealings with Corinth. Her importance in the busy port city, where she was clearly efficient (as *diakonos*) and able to champion Paul and "many" (as *prostatēs*) indicates that she would not be leaving that sphere unless she could perform important services in Rome. Was she going there on some errand of her own, while Paul just used this chance occurrence to send a letter along with her?

That idea does not fit in with the convergence of so many other important associates of Paul upon Rome. It has always puzzled people that Paul could send greetings to so many people with whom he had ties in a city he had not seen yet himself—twenty-five Brothers or Sisters already in Rome are named in the conclusion to his letter. These are not casual acquaintances. Two of them are, like Paul, emissaries. Three are "fellow workers in Messiah" with Paul. Four (all women) have been "hard workers" for the Lord. Two have been imprisoned with him. One is his protectress. One he calls "my mother too." Two are dearly loved friends (and one of these was "the first harvest for Messiah in Asia"). One (Apelles) is "tested in Messiah." Another (Rufus) is "the Lord's chosen one." This is a crack team, in effect the best possible muster of Paul's operatives who are free and able to join him when he gets to Rome.

Scholars are right to think that this assembly cannot be a mere chance gathering. But some of them draw the wrong conclusion. They believe that the list actually contains greetings Paul sent to other places as well as Rome (Ephesus is the top contender). The names became affixed to this letter by some accident. But there is good reason to think that Paul has assembled these people for a grand project, whose scale is suggested by the length and ambition of the letter that announces the project—his plan to take the revelation to Spain (Rom 15.20–24). Paul's operation has now reached a stage where he can coordinate the resources, skill, and dedication of many helpers to take on a vast new region, one that was very important in the Roman empire but where "Messiah's very name is unknown" (Rom 15.20).

Rome was to be the staging area for this vast endeavor. He means to raise support there while he mends his fences with Jerusalem, to anticipate and prevent any opposition or interference to the whole new front he is opening. As we shall see, he uses a dispute in Rome to recast the harsh rhetoric against Jerusalem employed by him during the earlier clash at Antioch. He no doubt hopes that the Romans will support him when they send their delegates with the collection for the needy. He will also circulate copies of this very letter in Judaea, through intermediaries and finally in person. Rome is the fulcrum on which he will balance what is, in effect, a "worldwide" reach, toward Jerusalem in the East and toward Spain in the West. Phoebe, Prisca, and her husband, along with the other members of Paul's assembled team, are to organize the elements for this campaign while Paul goes to solidify support in Jerusalem. It is all to be the climax of Paul's mission—one that is tragically cut short by the dark outcome of his eastward trip.

Women Prophets

PHOEBE WAS NOT the only woman of some resources giving support to Paul in Corinth. He heard reports of trouble there from traveling members of "Chloe's establishment"—literally, "they of Chloe" (1 Cor 1.11). Since Chloe herself did not send the report, it is supposed that she had some business or family at Corinth, and slaves or workers were traveling either to her or to her other holdings. Chloe was probably a well-to-do widow, like another businesswoman Luke mentions—Lydia, the dealer in precious dyes (Ac 16.14), who had a gathering at her house in Philippi (16.40).

The troubles reported by Chloe's establishment were deep and complex, as we shall see, and they afforded plenty of occasions for prophecy, the gift of the Spirit Paul lists just after that of emissaries. Prophecy is now popularly thought to mean prediction of the future. But the Jewish prophets were inspired denouncers of those who lapsed from the Lord's ways, reformers and purifiers. The faults of Corinth had their excoriaters, and *some of the prophets were women*. Paul writes that in the gatherings there a woman "should not pray *or prophesy* with her head uncovered" (1 Cor 11.5). He is addressing a squabble that had arisen about clothing in the gathering, but the important point for us to notice is that Paul takes it for granted that, bareheaded or not, women are prophets in the gathering. He is just as strict in saying that men should *not* have their heads covered when they pray or prophesy. Since we do not have the grounds for the departure from custom that was causing bitterness, we cannot say how serious they were, or what they were supposed to signify—

apparently the arrogantly spiritualist party was introducing a daring innovation. At any rate, Paul obviously thinks of them as deliberately offensive, and the cause of needless ridicule from outsiders. He says that the head covering is a "sign of authority for a woman in respect of the angels" (1 Cor 11.10)—who veil their faces before God (Is 6.2).

Though Paul is adjudicating a situation that is merely a matter of social practice, he backs up his argument on theological grounds that are sexist. Man can go uncovered because he is the direct image of God, while woman is the image of God's image—man—created after him and meant to be his helpmate (1 Cor 11.7–9). It was impossible for a man in that culture, patriarchal in both its Jewish and Roman societies, to shed every remnant of sexism. But the important thing is to notice that Paul gives every kind of honor to the women he works with—as emissaries, as prophets, as attendants *(diakonoi)*. They are not second-class citizens in the gatherings he knows or in the ideals he holds up for them.

If that is the case, how did Paul get a reputation for misogyny? He owes that principally to his impersonators and interpolaters. The supposedly Pauline letters, written late in the first century, reflect a church that is cutting back on the radical egalitarianism of its early days. Male church officers are emerging—married overseers *(episkopoi)* and deacons *(diakonoi)*—and patriarchy is being reimposed (1 Tim 3.1–7). The First Letter to Timothy is especially blunt in telling women to shut up: "A woman must be an entirely submissive learner. I forbid a woman to teach, or to take the lead over her husband— she should hold her peace" (1 Tim 2.11–12). But here there is a great objection to be made. In a letter universally admitted to be authentic, Paul also tells women to shut up:

> As in all gatherings of the Holy, women must be silent in the gatherings. They are not to speak up *(lalein)* but to be submissive, as custom dictates. If they would learn, let them seek knowledge from their husbands at home. It is a disgrace for a woman to speak up in the gathering. (1 Cor 14.34–35)

Earlier in this very letter, Paul had told women to cover their heads when speaking up and prophesying. Paul can be accused of contradicting himself, but not so blatantly in the confines of a single document. This fact has led a great many scholars to condemn this passage as an interpolation, added to the letter when the policy of the letter to Timothy had been adopted. The pseudo-Paul has intruded upon real Paul.

"As I Am"

SOME MAY SUSPECT Paul of misogyny since he is opposed to marriage. He writes that he would prefer that the unmarried remain that way, "as I am," saying that married people are busied with concern for each other, which can drain away concern for the Lord (1 Cor 7.32–34). Did Paul never marry? Even Catholic Bible scholars, like Jerome Murphy-O'Connor and Joseph Fitzmyer, think that highly unlikely. In the second century, Clement of Alexandria thought that Paul had been married but was separated from his wife, and other early authors held that view.[3] Apparently Paul was a mature man by the time the risen Lord appeared to him, and a Pharisee was usually obliged to marry. Paul was probably married in his twenties, though he is no longer by the time he writes. His wife could have died, left him, or been sent away under Jewish Law. Even in the new gatherings, he says that a nonbelieving spouse can be let go if that spouse is opposed to the religion of a believer (1 Cor 7.15).

Of course, Paul cannot make his opposition to marriage a requirement, since Peter and the brothers of the Lord traveled about with their wives (1 Cor 9.5). In the Brotherhood, marriage is the normal way of life, even for emissaries. In the later letters to Timothy and Titus, marriage is usual for "bishops" and "elders" (1 Tim 3.2, Tit 1.6). Thus Paul can only recommend his preference. He repeatedly emphasizes that this is not a teaching he has from the Lord.

> I give this as a recommendation, not a direction: I prefer
> that all men be as I am. But each has his own spiritual

gift *(charisma)* from God, so one will act this way, another that. (1 Cor 7.6–7)

This is I speaking, not the Lord. (1 Cor 7.12)

I have received from the Lord no requirement concerning virgins, but I offer my opinion as one in a position of trust by the mercy of the Lord. (1 Cor 7.25)

I suppose *(nomizo)*, then, that it is a good thing in this imminent crisis, that it is good for a man to remain in the same condition [neither to dissolve a marriage nor to undertake one]. (1 Cor 7.26)

I say this for your benefit, not to tie you up. (1 Cor 7.35)

This is just my opinion, though even I have the Spirit of God, too. (1 Cor 7.40)

In saying that he has no instruction from the Lord on celibacy, Paul either does not know the saying of Jesus about those "castrated for heaven's reign" or does not take it as an instruction. All that Jesus says in the Gospel is "Let one who can yield to *(chorein)* this, yield to it" (Mt 19.12). Paul's only reference to castration is a sardonic comment on enthusiasts for circumcision. If they are so intent on it, he says, they should cut off not only the foreskin but the whole member (Gal 5.12).

Paul's own opposition to marriage is not misogynist but eschatological. He is against women marrying as well as men, and that does not make him a misanthrope. His stand is part of his general social passivity. He says that slaves, though they may welcome freedom if it is given them, should not agitate for it (1 Cor 7.20–21). "As a person was when called by God, so let him continue" (7.24). In the same way, he is against political agitation or reform (Rom 13.1–7). The spread of the revelation is so pressing a duty, as history reaches its conclusion, that all else is to be considered a distraction from that single concern. Paul has enough trouble with the Roman authorities just in carrying out his mission. He does not want to get entangled in any other concerns.

> I tell you this, Brothers: the crisis impends. During what time is left, let those with wives be as if they had none, let those who mourn be as not [having time for] mourning, let those celebrating be as if not celebrating, let those who buy be as if not possessing, and those using this world be as if not using it. For the whole frame of this present order is about to go. (1 Cor 7.29–31)

In this eschatological context, Paul can imagine only one condition where he thinks marriage preferable—if one is so enflamed by passion that this in itself is a distraction from the work of the revelation: "Better to marry than to stay en-flamed" (1 Cor 7.9). Neither here nor elsewhere does Paul connect marriage with having children, the later Christian rationale. Since history is ending, the raising of children is no longer a concern in Paul's eyes. The only reference he makes to children is to say that the child of one Holy parent can be considered Holy, even if the other parent is a nonbeliever (1 Cor 7.14). Paul's frame of thought is far from what would be ascribed to him in the supposedly Pauline letters to Timothy and Titus, where the disciplining of bishops' children is addressed (1 Tim 3.4–5, Tit 1.6).

Despite Paul's preference, he himself gives evidence that married people were able to be intensely devoted to the Lord. Prisca even went to prison with him. In his Letter to the Romans, he names four married people who "worked hard" for the Lord. In Philippians, he adds another two, Euodia and Syntyche, who were his "fellows in the struggle" (Phil 4.3). Phoebe is his protectress. Another Sister is like his mother. Chloe's establishment keeps him informed. His crack team assembled in Rome for the Spanish campaign includes ten women, at least three of them married. He knows a woman emissary *(apostolos)*, a woman attendant *(diakonos)*, and women prophets. He knows two women leaders in Philippi, Euodia and Syntyche, who have become rivals, and he begs for their reconciliation (not their condemnation) at Philippians

4.2–3. The later misogyny of the Christian churches would never have occurred if the spirit of Paul had continued in them.

NOTES

1. Wayne Meeks, *The First Urban Christians: The Social World of the Apostle Paul*, second edition (Yale University Press, 2003), p. 132.

2. Ibid., pp. 20, 59.

3. Eusebius, *History of the Church* 3.30.1.

6. Paul and the Troubled Gatherings

☩

Six of Paul's seven recognizably authentic documents were addressed to gatherings with specific troubles. As John Gager puts it: "The circumstances under which Paul wrote all of his surviving letters, in modern terms we would call them attempts at damage control."[1] Some think that the last extant letter, to the Romans, is an exception to this statement, and others that the earliest letter, to the Thessalonians, is an at least partial exception. But there is good reason to think that they, too, fit under the same rule. I shall take them in the presumed chronological order.

Thessalonians

This is addressed to Thessalonica, the capital of northern Greece (Macedonia). I have already noticed that Luke in the Acts implies that Paul was run out of this community in a matter of weeks, and that Paul admits he was forced to leave by Jewish enmity. He says in the letter that the gathering there suffers from "straits" (*thlipsis*, 1 Thess 1.6). There is disagreement whether this means severe persecution or merely the difficulties that people who have left their own family and friends to take up a new discipline are bound to undergo. If Paul was expelled, why should the community he left behind be in peace? Besides, they are upset over those who have died since Paul was there, who may miss out on the Lord's Arrival *(Parousia)*. Can that many have died so soon without a persecution?

But if such a persecution had occurred, would Paul refer to it so vaguely as a generalized "pressure" *(thlipsis)*? The community seems to have been flourishing, since it has extended its influence over both parts of Greece, Macedonia and Achaea (1 Thess 1.7–8). Also, he says he has expected to return, and been prevented by things other than fear of further disturbance; and he sends Timothy without any expression of concern for his safety. His reference to reports on the Thessalonians' influence shows that he has been in communication with the place, not cut off or worrying about its fate.

Still, he does feel a need to send Timothy back, depriving himself of Timothy's important help. The mission he sends him on must be more than a way of sending his greetings. This letter is written as a response to Timothy's return, bringing reports that cheer Paul. But certain emphases in the letter indicate that there are sensitive matters to be dealt with. Why does Paul so pointedly stress how he and his fellows did hard manual work when they were in Thessalonica (1 Thess 2.9)?

We know that he also got help from Philippi while he was there. In Corinth and Rome, economic divisions in the gatherings caused tensions. Paul here seems to hint at a fear that the leaders of the community are now setting themselves apart from the working class or the poorer Brothers. He is probably admonishing those leaders, tactfully, when he urges the community to respect them: "We beg you, Brothers, to recognize those who *work so hard* for you and represent you in the Lord and advise you—give them generous esteem in your love for their *work*" (1 Thess 5.12–13). If the influence of Thessalonica has extended itself, it must be through the efforts of these leaders, but he is reminding them that they must earn their respect as he did by "night and day" labor for others.

The other notable thing about this letter has been noticed earlier, its first treatment of the end time in New Testament literature. The surface concern is that people worry about the fate of those who have died. This does not mean, necessarily, that a great number have actually perished since Paul's departure. The issue has obviously been debated in prospect. What concerns Paul is that different opinions are being offered (again diminishing the credibility of the leaders). That is why he brings his biggest weapon to bear—the Lord's own word (1 Thess 4.15). He is addressing not only an existential fear but a matter of doctrinal clarity. This is enough to show that even this "pastoral" letter had real controversial prompting.

Galatians

THERE IS NO DOUBT about the troubles prompting Paul to write his most polemical letter. It is the conflict between circumcised and uncircumcised Brothers, and it leads Paul to his most vitriolic comments, not only about the present antagonists, but about Peter and James in his earlier clash with them at Antioch. This is the letter that disconcerted Saint Jerome, and it became the model or excuse for reciprocal vilifications in the Reformation. The veracity of the early records of the faith is established by the fact that this letter was not suppressed. Paul later indicates that he came to regret the bitterness expressed here. He certainly did not follow his own counsel to others, that they correct each other with kindness. He takes an entirely different approach in his irenic Letter to the Romans.

Of course, we do not have the other side, which may have been just as intemperate. He could be trading taunt for taunt, fighting fire with fire. This is the only letter that is sent to a region, not to a single city. The circumcisionists (literally, "they of the circumcision") must have waged an aggressive campaign against Paul in several towns at once, and Paul sends a copy of his letter to each one. He says the Galatians are being bewitched by the agitators (3.1); they are tearing themselves apart (5.15). After dictating this tirade, he takes the pen himself to write the last paragraph: "Look at this large scrawl put down with my own hand" (6.11). The whole letter is a cri de coeur: "I wish I were already by your side, to modulate my tone, so frustrated am I" (4.20). He writhes with anxiety, as if in renewed birth pangs for his children (4.19). He is wounded and he means to wound others—even telling them to castrate themselves (5.12)—Raymond Brown wonders if the scribe hesitated to put those words down as Paul dictated them.

Philippians

PHILIPPI, in Northern Greece, was the first European town Paul reached. He must have approached this new arena with some apprehension, and he recalls with pride and pleasure the warm response he was given there by people who are "my joy, my crown" (4.1). Now he writes from prison (probably in Ephesus), wishing he were back among his early supporters. They have sent a representative, Epaphroditus, to cheer him up; but they were upset when they heard that Epaphroditus fell ill, so he is sending him back to them in recovered strength (2.25–30). He is also about to send Timothy, to add to their comfort (2.19–24). Paul is happy that the revelation is still being spread despite his imprisonment, though he regrets that some use that fact to cause division—presumably with the Jews, who are blamed for turning him over to the Romans (1.15–18). But he is concerned that the circumcisionists are at work among them, too—the "dogs," as he calls them (3.2). There are divisions in the community, even dividing his old "fellow strugglers," Euodia and Syntyche (4.2). To heal these troubles he quotes the great hymn he had shared with them, on Jesus' "emptying himself" (2.6–11).

Philemon

PAUL HAD the services of a scribe, even in prison. He needed this because he no doubt wrote more letters to gatherings than the ones that have been preserved. He must also have written many letters to individuals, though this is the only one that has been preserved, perhaps because it helped a man who became well known to the Brothers for the help he gave to Paul. The occasion for this letter is not trouble in a whole gathering but the trouble of one man who held a gathering of Brothers at his home (Phlm 2). One of Philemon's slaves has done something wrong, and he has gone to Paul to act as an intercessor with his owner (a common procedure in Roman law). While dealing with Paul, the slave, Onesimus, has performed some service for him, perhaps as a scribe writing this very letter, which he carries back to his owner. Roman slaves were often well-educated Greeks who acted as scribes, tutors, or bureaucrats, and Onesimus is a common Greek slave name, meaning "Useful." Paul puns on the meaning of the name when he tells Philemon that his slave was once unbeneficial (akhrēstos) to him but has now become beneficial (khrēstos) to both of them (Phlm 11).

Paul asks for special favors for this slave. He is not setting a general policy on slaves, or asking Philemon to free others of his household. It has been estimated that slaves made up as much as a quarter to a third of urban populations in Paul's time—he was not ready to work for the great social disruption of manumissions on that scale. We know that there were slaves in the gatherings of the Brothers, from Paul's advice that they accept their condition (1 Cor 7.20–21). He brought whole households (oikoi) into the faith together (1 Cor 1.16), and oikos usually meant the extended "family" of all dependents, including slaves. The term "Chloe's establishment" was probably meant to include slaves (1 Cor 1.11), as could the tent-making operations of Prisca and Aquila. Onesimus, however, was not brought to the faith as part of Philemon's household—Paul tells us that he became a Brother only in his own company (Phlm 16). The fact that he was not baptized with Philemon's oikos might seem surprising, since that was a family center active for the revelation. Paul greets Philemon himself as a "coworker" in the faith; his wife, Apphia, as a Sister; and another member of the household, Archippus, as having "soldiered with me" (Phlm 2).

The explanation that suggests itself is that Onesimus, as an educated slave, operated away from his master's oikos, perhaps taking care of his financial interests in another city, which took him close to Paul. Paul hints that the slave's crime was financial when he writes to Philemon:

If you and I are one, then think of him as me. If he has wronged you, or owes you, put that on my account. See, here I sign myself PAUL, that I will repay you—I will not mention that you owe your very self to me. Or, rather, Brother, put me in your debt and ease my anguish in Messiah. (Phlm 17–20)

Another puzzling thing about the letter is that Onesimus has had time to perform many and valuable services for Paul, which brought him so close to the prisoner that Paul now calls him "part of my very being" (literally, his "innards," *splagkhna,* Phlm 12), so that he is in "anguish" over the slave's fate (again, in his "innards," Phlm 20). If Onesimus went to Paul only to intercede with his master, why did Paul not send him back at once? I imagine that Onesimus, working for Philemon in Ephesus (if that is where Paul's prison was), had been told to perform services for Paul while continuing to do his master's business in that town. But in the course of dealing with Paul he came in time to accept the revelation, and only then confessed that he had been defrauding Philemon. Paul now sends him back to be reconciled with Philemon, hoping that he will be released into continued service with himself. If that was the outcome, as seems most likely, then the continued joint action of Paul and Onesimus would have made this event, and the letter accomplishing it, famous throughout the gatherings, insuring the preservation of the letter. It would hardly have been kept if all that eloquence had failed.

Corinthians

OF ALL THE GATHERINGS Paul addressed, those in Corinth were the most refractory. His dealings with them were sticky, thorny, and cantankerous. He stayed with them on three or more occasions (2 Cor 12.14, 13.1), sent personal assistants to them in his absence, received their delegations, and wrote them at least five letters, probably more, three or four or five of which are layered together in what have come down to us as two agglutinated letters. Factions spawned in Corinth. There were problems of doctrine, discipline, and vision, problems of class, of gender, of personalities. Paul was ridiculed there and he responded wrathfully, once in a wounding letter, once in a tearful one (these probably lost but leaving traces in what remains).

The community was divided over a marriage that was considered incestuous under Jewish Law—one of the Brothers had wed his father's widowed second wife (a woman who was no blood relative and may have been the new husband's own age or younger). Paul claims that this would not be allowed "even among the nations"—the Gentiles (1 Cor 5.1). He demands that the whole gathering, by its joint authority, with him present in spirit, drive the man out of the gathering. He is as solemn as can be about this: "All of you coming together in the name of the Lord Jesus, myself present in spirit, with the power of our Lord, turn such a man over to Satan for the destruction of his flesh, that his spirit may be rescued on the day of the Lord" (1 Cor 5.4–5). The baptized Brothers are one "in Messiah." To be outside Messiah is to be back in the realm of Satan, exposed to his ravages. Subject again to the law of the dying flesh (Paul seems to be saying), the man will strive back toward being in Messiah by the time Messiah comes. Some might well have thought Paul rather arbitrary in this proceeding, and we have difficulty understanding it until we look at the other clusters of misunderstanding in the place.

The main trouble in Corinth seems to have been a form of superspirituality. Like New Age types seeking fashionable preachers, some people became puffed up and "airy," saying their newest gurus (claiming to represent Apollos, for instance, or Peter) are higher minded than Paul (1 Cor 1.12, 3.22), that their own gifts of prophecy and speaking in tongues bring them closer to the Spirit than more ordinary folk, that they know of a better form of baptism (1 Cor 1.13–17). Paul calls the preachers of such attitudes high-flying emissaries—literally, the "super-too-much *(hyperlian)* emissaries" (2 Cor 11.5, 12.11), and repeatedly says that their followers are "inflated" *(physioi)* or self-inflated (1 Cor 4.18, 5.2, 8.1, 13.4). Krister Stendahl describes the high-flying emissaries as "slick operators."[2] Their women's newfangled way of prophesying (without headdress) is modishly "daring." Without disparaging spiritual gifts, and while saying he has experienced them himself, Paul reminds them that these are given for the good of the whole gathering, and that without love the spiritualists become as a resonating gong (prophecy?) or a jangling cymbal (speaking in tongues?).

While ironically calling high-minded people the "stronger" element in the gathering, Paul boasts of his own weakness (1 Cor 2.1–5, 2 Cor 12.7–10). He will admit that the stronger may have superior insight—for instance, since they realize that idols are a mere nothing, they can eat meat sacrificed to idols (1 Cor 8.4–6, 10.25–27). But Paul tells these high flyers to defer to "the weak," who still see some taint in that kind of food (1 Cor 8.7–13, 10.19–21, 28–33). Above all, he tells the strong not to draw themselves together to eat better things at the Lord's Meal, since that destroys the whole point of the union of Messiah being realized in their eating together (1 Cor 11.20–22). The lofty-souled seem to have done what later superspiritualists would, putting themselves above the observance of laws binding ordinary mortals. That is why Paul criticizes what seems to have been one of their mantras:

"Everything is permitted" (to the higher spirits; 1 Cor 6.12, 10.23). This may have been the point of the "strong" in saying that the marriage of a man to his stepmother, who lacked any blood tie, was permissible, though vulgar opinion held it to be incest. It is clearly why the high-flying emissaries said they were following the Lord's command in taking pay for their spiritual activities (1 Cor 9.14–18). The high flyers also seem to have thought they had already entered into the spiritual state of the glorified body. That is why Paul makes the odd point that they have to die first before they can live so exempt from earthly morals, and then their bodies will be so entirely different as to be unimaginable now (1 Cor 15.35–43).

By the time of the collection of texts cobbled together in what we call Second Corinthians, Paul must have realized that simple denunciation was not working. He was now looking for ways to compromise. When his very integrity was questioned, with regard to the Jerusalem fund's collection and security, he brought in neutral supervisors appointed by "the gatherings" (2 Cor 8.18–22). His account of his own spiritual gifts was a way of granting the validity of those in other people. He became autobiographical in order to forge ties with those making new claims for the Spirit. Grappling with the Corinthians was for him a harrowing struggle, one that makes for heady reading, even in the jumbled record it left behind.

Romans

THE LETTER to the Romans is the only one, extant and authentic, in which Paul does not mention cosenders (though he delivers it by way of Phoebe). It is the only one addressed to a place he had never seen, to gatherings that were formed before he even became a Brother. But it is also his longest and most theologically ambitious letter. Some think that the lack of a troubled community within his own experience freed him to a more leisurely exposition of basic themes. But that plays down the fact that he had received reports of a way in which the Roman gatherings *were* troubled. He may have exaggerated the trouble for his own purposes, since it gave him a chance to rework an earlier stand he had come to regret. But more important, it gave him the opportunity to address the *Jerusalem* Brothers without direct confrontation or solicitation of a good opinion.

He clearly wanted copies of this letter to be seen in Jerusalem—and probably elsewhere. Some copies he would take with him, others he hoped his team in Rome would circulate there before his arrival and encourage Roman Brothers to send on to their friends and allies in Jerusalem. One of the reasons Paul needed scribes was to produce multiple copies of his letters, for his own records and to verify the copies others would make of them. Before the age of printing, an author "published" only by having the same text laboriously copied out over and over. The letter to Rome was a production Paul took great pains over. Its rhetoric is highly wrought, its argument dense and ingenious. It is not a calm summary of his thinking, but an intense engagement with his Jewish past and his offended brethren. It is peppered with those heckling rhetorical questions characteristic of diatribe. It is a careful beginning to his last and largest campaign.

The trouble in Rome, however unfortunate for those experiencing it, was perfect for Paul's needs. It was the same conflict that had made him erupt in Antioch, a division in the gathering over Jewish food laws. But the dynamics had shifted. In Antioch, the "Judaizers" had the upper hand, while the Gentile Brothers were the innovators, suspect and easily intimidated by pressures emanating from Jerusalem. Paul became absolutist in that situation, telling Peter that he was nullifying the freedom of Christ as he insisted on kosher discipline. Paul called any compromise at that point a form of "hypocrisy," and his stand made him temporarily lose his partner Barnabas and break off his efforts to raise the Jerusalem fund in Antioch. Now, however, writing to the Romans, Paul argues for tolerance and reconciliation. Partly this reflects the shift in dynamics just mentioned. In Rome, it is the Gentile Brothers who have the upper hand and are intimidating the Jewish Brothers. What makes this possible is a break in the social continuity of Jewish life not experienced elsewhere, one caused by the emperor Claudius.

In his *Life of Claudius* (25.4), the Roman historian Suetonius records that the emperor "expelled from Rome the Jews because of continual disturbances provoked by Chrestus." It is universally held that Suetonius misunderstood the title *Christus*, an odd term for a Roman, as a proper name, and assimilated it to a name that was common at the time, Chrestus (from Greek *Khrēstos*. "Worthy" or "Beneficial"). By 49 CE, in other words, there was a sizable enough community of the Brothers in Rome to create dissension in the Jewish community over something connected with "Chrestus," and the emperor, without getting into the causes or sorting out who was really involved, solved the problem by throwing out the whole lot. Jews, whether Brothers or not, were expelled from the city.

It is easy to reconstruct what happened, since it had parallels throughout the Empire, ones that brought Paul and others before Roman tribunals. Jews had good reason to fear and resent the Brothers. They had worked out a cautious and precarious modus vivendi with the Roman authorities, one in which they were tolerated and even protected, despite resentment of their separatist ways, their different holidays, their abstention from pagan feasts, their private food supplies and preparations. The Brothers disturbed this delicate situation, dividing

Jewish family members by their departures from the Law, and luring the Reverent (the *Theosebeis*) away from them. These important Gentile friends and patrons were a source of protection, of political and financial support, for the endangered Jewish minorities. It was necessary for Jews to represent the Brothers as not authentic participants in the allowed space earned and confirmed by Jews over the years. The Brothers, they would say, were more like the odd and menacing "new" religions from the East that Romans considered disruptive and a menace to Rome's cults. Jews therefore appealed to the Roman authorities they had cultivated, asking them to prevent disruption in the Jewish community caused by the Brothers. The "disturbances" that Claudius punished need have been no more than the nuisance of repeated attempts to involve Roman courts in religious squabbles.

When the Jews were cast out of Rome, Jewish Brothers would not have been distinguished from those not involved in "Chrestus." According to Luke, Prisca and Aquila were among the Jewish Brothers who had to leave Rome, and who ended up in Corinth, where they met Paul (Ac 18.2). But most of the Jews from Rome were likely to stay near the networks they had formed in Italy, holding together their communities in exile, maintaining synagogue organizations and economic relations with the surrounding country. When, in 55 CE, Claudius died, they were able to return with social structures intact, to reclaim properties they had leased or committed to friendly Romans, resuming the pattern of their lives within the old guarantees.

The Jewish Brothers would have returned as well, but to a new situation. The Gentile Brothers, who were not covered by the decree, had for six years been able to expand their own community without any harassment from the synagogues—a unique occurrence in the early history of the Brotherhood.[3] Returning Jewish Brothers would now be the outsiders in their own surroundings. Those who had maintained their ties to the Jewish Law would find little sympathy for their ways in gatherings that had lived with only minimal connections to the Jewish origins of Jesus.

Paul's letter is an impassioned assertion that those connections can never be severed. It used to be thought that the recipients of the letter were made up mainly of Jewish Brothers, since Paul argues at length and learnedly from intimate acquaintance with Jewish scripture. But the reason for this is just the opposite of what was then supposed. He stresses the Jewish foundations because they are so *little* familiar to the one community of Brothers who had been isolated for a time from that past. It will be seen how useful this argument was for approaching the Brothers he was about to see again in Jerusalem. He was making it clear that his mission to the nations was not a separate endeavor, unrelated to the lives and history of Jewish Brothers, or unrelated to the calling of the whole Jewish people in their uncanceled covenant with God.

Paul's main task is to tell the Gentile Brothers that God's promise to the Jewish people is not broken—it cannot be broken. He devotes most of the first thirteen chapters (as we now know them) to this thesis. Only in chapters fourteen and fifteen does he get around to the observation of food codes in Rome. It is not surprising, then, that commentators have seen these late chapters as a mere addendum to the large-scale argument preceding them. But that long discussion was a careful way of sorting out the problem of the community he was addressing. Admittedly, he went beyond the immediate issue, which was the relation of Gentile to Jewish Brothers, and addressed the relation of all Brothers to all the Jews. But this added an a fortiori power to his argument in the immediate situation. If the Brothers must recognize God's unbreakable commitment to the whole Jewish people, *how much more* must they see the reason for Brothers to honor their ties to the people God first chose.

When it comes to the actual situation in Rome, Paul does not go back to the clash in Antioch, where he was for an absolute break with certain provisions of the Mosaic Law, but to Corinth, where he talked of a strong party and a weak one. Here, too, he says that the strong party may have the more defensible reason for its "freedom," but a regard for the united body of the Lord must make it defer to the fears of the "weak" members. In Corinth, the strong party saw no problem in eating meat killed for idols. In Rome, the strong party

sees no problem in eating meat not killed to the kosher requirements. The case might seem less urgent in Rome, but
Paul makes it more symbolically important. Admittedly, a
higher principle is involved—that *nothing* is unclean in itself,
not merely things directly connected with idolatry—but a
more urgent priority is at stake on the actual scene: regard for
the Jewish roots of the Brotherhood. Where once he had exco-
riated Peter for insisting on the food code, now he tells Romans to accept it out of regard for tender consciences:

If your Brother takes offense with you over the food being eaten, it is because you are not observing the love
you should walk in with him. Do not put his soul at stake
over your food observance—Christ died for him. What
you see as good should not be another's reproach. God's
reign is not a matter of food or drink, but of God's vindication, of peace, of joy in the Holy Spirit. Messiah's slave
in these matters is the one loved of God and favored of
men. Let us then seek peace and the mutual upbuilding
of each other. Why use food to block God's own project?
Nothing is unclean of itself. But the individual may
wince at one form of eating. Some find it best not to eat
meat, or drink wine, or to do anything that a Brother
finds offensive. If you, however, are assured in doing
these things, keep it a matter of confidence with God.
Happy the person who can act out of assurance, and
one who acts against his own principles in eating is

self-convicting, not keeping his integrity, for anyone who is not in accord with himself is in the wrong. Still, we who are confident should favor the weakness of those who are not confident, not trying to coerce them. Each should defer to the other, to strengthen the structure of the whole gathering, since Messiah himself gave way to others. (Rom 14.15–15.3)

Paul would have been far better off if he had taken this stand in Antioch. But he should be credited with the fact that he reached it in time. One of the ways he teaches us is by learning himself. We find out what Paul meant by seeing how he eventually came closer to what Jesus meant.

NOTES

1. John G. Gager, *Reinventing Paul* (Oxford University Press, 2000), p. 77.

2. Krister Stendahl, *Paul Among Jews and Gentiles* (Fortress Press, 1976), p. 47.

3. James C. Walters, *Ethnic Issues in Paul's Letter to the Romans* (Trinity Press International, 1993).

7. Paul and Jews

✝

IT HAS LONG and often been alleged that Paul is a father of Christian anti-Semitism. Where does he stand on the staples of that vile record? Take two of these. First, did he call the Jews Jesus-killers? Second, did he say that Jews are cursed by God?

On the killing of Jesus, he first denies that the Jews did it. "Not a single one of the rulers of the world knew this [the revelation]. Had they known, they would not have crucified the Lord of splendor" (1 Cor 2.8). The Jews were not the rulers of the world when Jesus was killed. They were themselves ruled by the rulers of the world, the Romans, who killed Jesus. On the other hand, Paul does say that the same Jews who killed earlier prophets also killed Jesus. Writing to the Thessalonians, he says:

> You, Brothers, have repeated what happened to God's Judaean gatherings that were in Messiah-Jesus, since you have suffered from your own kinsmen what they did from the Jews, who killed the Lord and the prophets—the same who drove us away from you, displeasing God and opposing all men by preventing us from telling the

nations how they are rescued, which completes their account of guilt over all time, anticipating the last anger against them. (1 Thess 2.14–16)

This is the greatest proof text in the authentic letters for Paul's anti-Semitism. Some argue that it, like the passage telling Corinthian women to shut up, is an interpolation by later people with later attitudes, and there are some oddities about the text that might help them in their claim. But the effort to get rid of the passage is too clearly a matter of wishful thinking. The matter must be considered later.

On the second point, did Paul say that God cursed the Jews? Definitely not: "I tell you: Has God repudiated his own people? Far from it!" (Rom 11.1). How could they be his own people if he repudiated them? On the other hand, Paul wrote: "Those who act under the Law are under a curse" (Gal 3.10).

How is one to reconcile such divergent statements? A first reaction may be to say that this was one crazy mixed-up Jew—and that may, in fact, be the beginning of wisdom. It may free us from the false starting point so many take with Paul—one assuming that that he left Judaism to join and promote a different religion, the Christian church, pitting the latter against the former. But there was no such entity in his time as a Christian church. There were only Jews who saw Jesus as the promised Messiah of the Jews and, supplementarily, Gentiles who saw Jesus as the promised Messiah of the Jews, who were the people Paul was sent to call in. He teaches his followers from nothing but the Jewish scriptures, and presents the Messiah as the fulfillment of the Jewish covenant. We thus have a continuum between three groups:

1. Jews not accepting Jesus as the Messiah of the Jews
2. Jews accepting Jesus as the Messiah of the Jews
3. Non-Jews accepting Jesus as the Messiah of the Jews

There is no one here outside a Jewish context, no group to be opposed to the Jews as a whole. There are only divisions within the Jewish understanding of Yahweh. What we have is a family quarrel.

Paul never presents Jesus as the God of the Greeks, as the Wisdom of Plato, as the Unmoved Mover of Aristotle. He never quotes a passage or an argument about God from pagan philosophers or non-Jewish authors. (Luke makes him do that once—but Paul never does it in his own writings.) Paul's Gentile Brothers are instructed over and over in the intricacies of Jewish history and prophecy. They are told that *they* are the seed of Abraham, and told in detail why this is so (Rom 4.1–17). The prophets foretold their rescue—Paul calls the roll of them (Rom 15.9–12). For Paul there was no such thing as "the Old Testament." If he had known that his writings would be incorporated into something called the New Testament, he would have repudiated that if it was meant in any way to repudiate, or subordinate, the only scripture he knew, the only word of God he recognized, his Bible.

One of the most basic problems in reading Paul is knowing what he means when he refers to "Jews." People repeatedly mistake him as referring to the Jews of the number 1 group (page 127) when he is talking about those listed as number 2. The latter are the ones he has continuing contact and conflict with, as they try to impose Jewish Law on their Gentile brothers. Thus, when he says that Jews are "preventing us from telling the nations how they are rescued," he is referring to people like the "circumcisionists," or those imposing the Jewish food code *on Brothers*. Those are the adversaries that "dog" him from Antioch to Philippi (Phil 3.2). They precede him into Rome. In fact, as we shall see, it will be the Jewish Brothers who betray Paul to Nero for execution. Paul's harshest words about his fellow Jews are about his fellow *Brother Jews*, the ones who would later be called Christians. These are the ones he calls hypocrites (including Peter and James and Barnabas) and dogs (Gal 2.13, Phil 3.2). These are the ones he calls "damned" *(anathema)* in his anger against them (Gal 1.8–9).

That is enough to make us go back and look at the proof text for his anti-Semitism (1 Thess 2.14–16). Clearly in that passage the ones who are preventing the spread of the revelation to Gentiles are the *Brother* Jews. Are they the ones killing Jesus and the prophets? Not in the sense that the "rulers of the world" did at the crucifixion, but Paul sees the life of Jesus as his continuing presence in the body of the believers. Those who oppose him there are trying to kill him, as they did the prophets who proclaim the risen Lord (Paul among them). They are the ones who are "completing an account of guilt." If anyone thinks this is too strong a thing to say about Paul's fellow believers in Jesus, what do they make of his calling his fellow believers hypocrites and dogs and damned? These are ones who will turn Paul—and Peter as well—over for execution.

It would, in fact, make more sense to call Paul an anti-Jewish-Christian polemicist than an anti-Semite. But in any case there is no more Semitic a Semite than Paul. "If one relies on lineage, I can do so more than others—circumcised on the eighth day, by race a man of Israel, by tribe of Benjamin, Hebrew from Hebrews, in Law a Pharisee, in dedication a persecutor of the gathering, in vindication under the Law a man faultless" (1 Phil 3.4–6). "For Jewishness I outstripped many contemporaries of my own lineage, extreme in my jealous preservation of the patriarchs' traditions" (Gal 1.14). Paul is just as Jewish as Jewish can be. "I, after all, am an Israelite, of Abraham's seed, of Benjamin's tribe. God has not repudiated our people, recognized as his from the outset" (Rom 11.1–2). He cannot say it often enough or emphatically enough. "I could prefer to be outcast from Messiah myself if it would help my brothers, the forebears of my flesh, who are the Israelites. Theirs is the sonship, and the splendor, and the covenants, and the gift of Law, and the rites, and the promises. From them are the patriarchs, and from them, by fleshly descent, is the Messiah, the God above all, may he ever be praised. Amen" (Rome 9.3–5). Paul never boasts, as Luke makes him boast, of being a Roman citizen. He never boasts of coming from "a city of some note" (Ac 21.39). He boasts only of his Jewish roots and observance.

Then how, it is asked, can he attack the Jewish Law?

To be brief, he doesn't.

The Letter to the Romans, often taken to be Paul's central statement of doctrine, is usually misread because of the confusion of the three meanings of "Jews" already listed. It is thought to contrast the number 1 group of Jews with a fictive entity, Christianity. Actually, as I argued in the last chapter, Paul was addressing the number 3 group of Jews (Gentile believers in the Jewish Messiah), saying that they should defer to the scruples of the number 2 group in Rome, a minority of the Brothers in Rome. But this meant that he was speaking over the heads of number 3 Jews to number 2 ones (the Jewish Brothers who are to be accepted). And he is speaking over *their* heads to the Brothers in Jerusalem, whom he expects to read this letter, assuring them that he has not lost touch with their concerns. He is even speaking over the latter heads to the number 1 group, of Jews not yet accepting Jesus as the Messiah, saying that to do so is not to show disrespect for the Mosaic Law.

All this interplay of audiences is made possible, but also complicated, by the diatribe technique in this letter, the voicing of various views by various assumed personae. The complex relations thus set up are trampled into indistinguishable muddle by those who say Paul was attacking "Jewish Law" from the standpoint of "Christianity." And that simplism is further simplified by those who think he is attacking "law" or "works" in general from the standpoint of "faith" as a means of "justification" (the Lutheran reading at the very heart of Protestantism). All such approaches misread the first and obvious intent of the letter, which was to reconcile all groups of Jews, telling them not to judge one another (Rom 2.1), since God, who plays no favorites (2.11), is on the side of them all: "There is no distinction between Jew and Gentile, since there is only one Lord over all, profuse toward all who call on him, and all who call on the Lord's name will be rescued" (10.12).

The important first thing to notice about the letter is that when Paul speaks of moving beyond God's Law he is speaking of two laws laid down by God—not only the Jewish Law given to Moses, but the natural law given to Gentiles. He contrasts both *laws* with a single *promise* given to *both* Jews and Gentiles, the promise to Abraham that he would be the father of many nations (4.13). Jesus moves beyond both *laws* by being the fulfillment of the single *promise*.

The law given to the Gentiles is graven not on stone tablets but in their hearts: "From the universe's framing, men have perceived his unseen attributes, knowable from what he has done—his boundless power and divinity. This left them no excuse, when, despite knowing there is a God, they did not acknowledge his splendor and give thanks for it" (1.20–21). "Even when not expressly given law, the nations acknowledge the law, finding, even without law, a kind of law in themselves—those at any rate who show the effects of law written in their hearts, calling conscience as their witness when they argue with each other over whether this party is wrong, that party right—against the day when God will sift the secret things of man, according to the revelation I bring, in Messiah-Jesus" (2.14–16). But simply knowing natural law does not make men follow nature. The Gentiles are, as a whole, sinners. Proud of their philosophy, they proved fools (1.22).

Nor does having God's express Law make Jews follow it. On the contrary, as prophet after prophet assured them, the Jews are a rebellious people (10.21)—and their rebellion brings dishonor on God's name among the Gentiles (2.24). God punishes the offenders against both laws, natural law and covenant Law, the Jews in the first place, since the Law was their special possession to honor, but also the Gentiles (2.10)—just as he chose in the first place the Jews, but also the Gentiles (1.16). "Are we Jews ahead? Not entirely. We have seen the single sentence against all of us, Jew and Gentile, for the reign of sin, just as scripture tells us, 'None, not one, is vindicated.'" (3.9–10). To shame the Jews, God has called in the Gentiles to share the blessings promised to Jews. He is using the Gentiles, as he used Pharaoh (9.17), to correct the Jews. For they will be corrected. Their defection is only temporary.

> I say they have been tripped up. Does that mean they have fallen? Far from it. Their tripping means rescue for the Gentiles, to stimulate the Jews to compete. If their tripping up enriches the rest of the universe, if their loss is the Gentiles' gain, how much greater will be their own restored gain. If their lapse has meant the winning over of the universe, what can their restoration mean but life rising up from death? (11.11, 15)

As Krister Stendahl puts it, the Letter to the Romans is about God's cosmic "traffic plan." The Jews have been put "on hold," to bring the Gentiles up to speed. "The Jews in God's plan had to step aside for a little while so that the Gentiles had time to come in."[1] This is God's surprise way of completing the promise issued in the first place:

> All Israel will be rescued, as scripture says: "Out of Zion comes the Rescuer, to rip away iniquities from Jacob, so my covenant abides with them, to remedy their sinfulness." (11.26–27)

Paul says that it is necessary to honor the Jewish Law, even though Gentiles are not required to observe all its ceremonial requirements. He even says that "Jesus is an attendant *(diakonos)* on circumcision" (Rom 15.8). Why is Paul making these points to the Romans? Remember the situation he is addressing, where the Gentile Brothers are receiving back the Jewish Brothers, after the Claudian expulsion ended. Some Gentile Brothers were not honoring the Jewish Brothers' wish to keep up their observance of the Law. Paul has to remind the Gentile Brothers that the promises fulfilled by Jesus are *Jewish* promises, and the memory of the promise was passed down under the protection of the Law. "Has circumcision any use at all? It matters a great deal, chiefly because they were the custodians of the pronouncements of God" (3.1–2). Gentiles must acknowledge that the Mosaic Law was the custodian ("pedagogue" he calls it at Galatians 3.24) of the revelation that Jesus fulfills. Gentiles are grafted on to the Jewish trunk. But for that trunk, they would be floating in air, unconnected with God's design for the world and its rescue. This reminder to the Gentile Brothers is rightly called by Stendahl the first and best warning against what would become Christian anti-Semitism:

Some branches have been stripped away, and you, an alien olive branch, have been grafted on in their place and have taken on the life of the olive tree's original root—

which is no reason to crow over the replaced branches. However you may crow, you do not support the root—it supports you. Do you boast that those branches were stripped away to graft you in? Exactly. They were stripped away because they betrayed their trust. That is no reason for your elation, but for apprehension. If God did not spare those natural growths, why should he spare you? Consider God's beneficence, but also his rigor. His rigor was exercised against those who failed, and his beneficence toward you, provided you retain his beneficence, lest you too be cut away. And they will be grafted on again if they do not continue betraying their trust—it is easy for God to graft them on again, since you were unnaturally grafted when torn from an alien stock, but he can far more naturally graft them back on to their native tree.

I would impress this secret providence on you, Brothers, to keep you from confidence in your own conceit—that part of Israel has lost its vision, but only until the full number of Gentiles is brought in. Then all Israel will be rescued, as scripture says: "Out of Zion comes the Rescuer, to rip away iniquities from Jacob, so my covenant abides with them, to remedy their sinfulness." They are now foes to the revelation for your sake, but by their singling out they are the patriarchs' favored sons. God does not go back on what he gave them, they are his chosen ones. As you were outside the trust in God but are now spared, their betrayal of trust leads to your being spared—

but they will be spared in their turn. God provides for the betrayal of all to bring about the sparing of all. (11.17–32)

This optimism about God's inclusive plan hardly reflects the dark views of election, justification, and predestination that have been wrested out of the letter to the Romans. This is a letter of consolation and reconciliation: Paul did not think in terms of individual souls damned but of the rescue of whole peoples—indeed of the whole cosmos.

I would not count the suffering of this present order as at all comparable with the splendor that is to be unveiled for the offspring of God. The very frame of things is giddy with apprehension at what will be unveiled for the sons of God. The frame of things has been baffled, despite itself, by the one constraining it—yet with hope, since the whole frame will be liberated from its imprisoning decay, freed into the splendor of God's offspring. All this frame of things, we realize, has been moaning in the throes of some birth—and we, moreover, though we have the first harvest of the Spirit, moan along with it, yearning for full adoption as heirs and for the release of our bodies, saved by our trust. (8.18–24)

Even after some people admit the inclusiveness of Paul's hopeful vision for all peoples, they misunderstand him in any number of ways. To list just three:

1. Some think that he says the conversion of the Jews must precede the end of the world. But that would be grafting the trunk onto the branches. Paul speaks of the Brothers as joined to the Jewish promise, history, and fate, not vice versa. As Krister Stendahl says, Paul always thought of Gentiles as "honorary Jews."[2] How the original Jews and the honorary ones will be united at the climax of time is a mystery Paul leaves to God for accomplishment. He talks always of God's initiative, not man's. He does not know how the promise will be fulfilled, only that it will be, since God is the promiser. God's word must and will be kept. He never goes back on a promise (Rom 11.29). It is his responsibility. Our job is to trust in that word. "Does their betrayal of trust legitimate God's betraying his trust? Far from it. God will prove true though all men lie. As scripture has it: 'Whatever charge is brought against you, you are vindicated, in every judicial proceeding you prevail' " (3.4). "Has God rejected his own people? Far from it" (11.1).

2. Others have argued that Paul, since he does not see God canceling the Jewish Law, believes in a "two-track" rescue of mankind. Gentiles will believe in Jesus and Jews will stay with their Law, and only Gentiles will be rescued by Jesus. But Paul does not ever see Jesus as separate from the Jewish covenant and its fulfillment. Later generations would talk of conversion to Jesus as to a

separate religion, that of "the New Testament." It cannot be repeated often enough that Paul knew of no New Testament, and no rescue but that of the promise given to the Jewish people. He did not believe in a substitution of a new way to be rescued. He did believe, with Jesus, that the claims of the prophets had to be fulfilled, making a religion of the heart replace that of external observances. But he retained the core value of the Jewish Law, as both Jesus and he affirmed it. "The entire Law is fulfilled in this one saying, Love your neighbor as yourself" (Gal 5.14). "This is the Law and the prophets" (Mt 7.12). Modern Jews no longer believe in the observance of animal sacrifice. Paul said that circumcision was a great advantage, since it was the seal on the promise to Abraham. Though the promise was given before the seal was affixed to it (4.12), Jewish Brothers are right to observe the seal as a symbol of the promise. In the same way, Paul tells the Romans to defer to the Jewish Brothers who observe the food code, since that reaffirms the historic tie to God's covenant with his people. Nonetheless, Jesus is the fulfillment of the Jewish scripture, not of some separate revelation. Jesus believed in a religion of the heart that would oppose later Christian religious observance as much as any Jewish ceremonies. Jesus founded no new religion, and Paul preached none.

3. A deeper misunderstanding of Paul's inclusiveness

would move off entirely from the Jewish-Gentile issue. It turns the contrasts between a religion of the heart and that of the external purity code into Luther's contrast between faith and works. Luther said that faith in God alone "justifies" a person, apart from any virtuous acts. Paul was saying that observing external acts—like circumcision, prescribed holy days, and kosher law—is not a substitute for the internal acts of the Law, for love of God and one's neighbor. He calls this interior observance a "circumcision of the heart" (Rom 2.29). Paul criticized as sinners those Jews who departed from this internal law, just as he criticized Gentiles who departed from the natural law given them by God.

Luther was thinking in terms of the internal struggle of the individual sinner, not of the rescue of whole peoples, as Paul did—and as a prominent Lutheran bishop like Krister Stendahl does. Paul saw God's plan as dealing "wholesale," not retail. He was in a race with history, on his way to Spain, recruiting Romans in his effort to cover the whole Gentile world while he went back to bring the Jewish Brothers "on board" this mission. He was counting on the Jewish Brothers to bring their countrymen to a realization that Jesus is the one they had been promised and were still hoping for. His message was always of and for his—and Jesus'—blood kin.

NOTES

1. Krister Stendahl, *Final Account: Paul's Letter to the Romans* (Fortress Press, 1995), pp. 6–7.

2. Krister Stendahl, *Paul Among Jews and Gentiles* (Fortress Press, 1976), p. 37.

8. Paul and Jerusalem

✝

PAUL'S CONTINUING STRUGGLE with the Jerusalem church is made clear in his concern to fulfill what he agreed to in his first clash with it—that he should "keep in mind the needy" of Jerusalem. Much of the extant letters is devoted to making up the great fund for Jerusalem, a matter that became an obsession with him. He saw the collection as a bridge to the Jewish Brothers in Judaea, and even perhaps to the whole body of Jews. He was organizing the collection on a grand scale, one to rival the immense Temple tax payments that poured into Jerusalem annually from the millions of Diaspora Jews. He told the Corinthians how they could accumulate a considerable sum.

With regard to the collection for the Holy, you should follow the procedures I arranged in the Galatian gathering. Every Sabbath you should lay aside for saving some portion of your income, so it need not all be raised when I come. Once I am with you, I shall send representatives chosen by you with letters to carry your spontaneous favor *(charis)* to Jerusalem, myself going with them if that seems best. (1 Cor 16.1–4)

It became a massive operation. Each Diaspora gathering of the Brothers was to send a number of representatives with its offering. Paul was waiting to see whether his presence among them would be helpful or not—he had reason to worry about that. The result could be seen as a visible knitting together of the whole body of Jesus, in reciprocal care of each member for all others. Or might it be seen, and possibly resented, as a demonstration of the great superiority of numbers in the Diaspora Brotherhood over the Jerusalem gathering? With such a large-scale activity, might his foes suspect that Paul was trying to equal, perhaps to surpass, even to ridicule, the Temple tax that observant Jews sent? Paul will worry at such issues as he devotes increasing energy to his great scheme.

In his troubled later correspondence with the Corinthians, the collection has become hostage to the multiple misunderstandings in that city's gatherings. In an atmosphere of spreading distrust, questions have arisen about the safe and honest collecting of such a large sum. To deal with the controversy, Paul has asked the gatherings to choose neutral overseers of the collection, who will collaborate with Titus, the man the Corinthians accepted as Paul's spokesperson. Titus has been collecting sums in Macedonia, which—though the region is not as wealthy as Corinth—has proved spectacularly generous. Now Paul tries to coax the Corinthians, who are resisting, into at least matching the Macedonian contributions:

We have asked Titus, who set in motion this spontaneous favor from you, to bring it to fulfillment. Abounding as you do in faith, profession, love, and in every great effort—as well as in the love we share—abound as well in this spontaneous favor. I issue no order here. By mentioning the effort of others, I would impress them with the soundness of your love. You are aware how our Lord, Jesus-Messiah, has favored you, how from being rich he became poor for you, that his poverty might enrich you. My opinion on this is all I can give you, which is for your advantage. You yourselves led the way last year, not only by your actions but in your eagerness to act. Now you should complete what you began, matching your desire to give with actual giving, according to your means. The desire is approved if one gives within one's means, not beyond them. Relief of the Holy should not come from your deprivation, but a balance should be struck between your present having and their want, so that one day their having may supply your want, balancing things out, according to scripture: "The one taking much [of manna in the desert] did not have too much, nor did the one taking little have too little." (2 Cor 8.6–15)

For Paul, this interplay of giving and receiving among the gatherings was just the material expression of members' reciprocity in the body of Jesus:

For God has tempered all parts of the body, giving special attention to the lesser parts, to prevent internal division of the body with itself, all taking a common care of one another, so that if one part grieves they all grieve, and if one part thrives, they all take pride in it. You are Messiah's body, each part having its role. (1 Cor 12.24–26)

After Paul has decided to lead the delegations with their offerings toward Jerusalem, he informs the Romans (whom he has not yet visited) of his plan. Before, he had talked of balancing present giving with future receiving, as if Jerusalem might one day have a material surplus to render back to the Diaspora gatherings. Now he talks of a *simultaneous* balance to be struck between material giving and spiritual receiving. Jerusalem has already given the riches of its Jewish legacy to Diaspora gatherings, the promise of the covenant and the heritage of the prophets fulfilled in the life of Messiah. This is the most direct tribute he has ever paid to the Jerusalem Brothers. (As we have said, he means for the Jerusalem gathering to read these words.)

At this moment I am off for Jerusalem, in service to the Holy there, since Macedonia and Achaia have decided to express their oneness with the needs of the Holy in Jerusalem. They decided this out of a feeling of indebtedness to them. Since the nations were at one with the spiritual gifts of the Holy there, they thought it right to minister to their material needs. When I have finished with this, and sealed my part in their endeavor, I will stop by with you on my way to Spain. (Rom 15.25–28)

Despite his confidence about a mission to Spain, he betrays his uneasiness over the Jerusalem trip:

But I entreat you by our Lord, Jesus-Messiah, and by the love of the Spirit, take part in my ordeal by praying to God for me, that I may escape the rejectionists in Judaea, and that my service to Jerusalem may be taken in good part by the Holy there, that I may reach you in good spirits by the will of God, and be tranquil in your company. (Rom 15.30–33)

He has two concerns, his physical safety among the rejection-ists (*apeithountes*, literally the "unpersuaded") and his spiri-tual acceptance by the Jerusalem Brothers.

Paul's relations with the Jerusalem Brothers, for all Luke's efforts to disguise the fact, were always strained when not downright hostile. But if this was the case, why did Paul risk a dangerous trip there? He had earlier said that the delegates from the various cities might go without him. With the mis-givings he expressed to the Romans, why did he change his mind? We have to remember that he was planning to take the revelation to a whole new level of expansion, using Rome as a base to go into Spain. The roving emissaries of Jerusalem and the other gatherings posed a threat to unity he would not want to leave behind him. His long Letter to the Romans sets up a kind of fulcrum on which he wants to unite the new areas with the old. His long efforts in different cities to raise the collection were a continuing assurance to the old center that he was not forgetting them, cutting himself off, launching into the unknown with no umbilical cord back to the center— not only to Jerusalem, but to cities in close contact with it, and to groups within all the gatherings that circulated Brothers back to the city of the Temple and of Jesus' death and resurrection. Paul no doubt hoped that he was doing repair work on relations with Jerusalem, not only in the climax of his effort, the actual journey there, but in the well-publicized activity he and his team members were engaged in throughout the Diaspora to "keep in mind the needy" of Jerusalem.

After this dramatic buildup for the delivery of the great collection, we topple over into an abyss of silence about the collection's ultimate fate. Paul can tell us no more (Romans is counted his last extant letter) and Luke, if he knew what happened to the great sum, is not going to let us in on it. He brings Paul to an audience with James, where the collection is not mentioned (Ac 21.18–25). James warns Paul against enmity in the circumcised Brotherhood, and tells him he can defuse this by paying the Temple expenses of four members of the Nazarite (oath-taking) community. But in Luke's version of things the advice of James backfires. Some Jews seize on

Paul's presence in the Temple to claim that he contaminated it with Gentile associates. They arrest him and prepare to execute him (raising that old Luke problem of Jewish jurisdiction over capital punishment) when Roman soldiers intervene. The Romans are about to flog Paul when he claims that they are not allowed to beat a Roman citizen (Ac 22.25). Where, in this flurry of activity, has the collection gone? We do not know. But scholars are probably right in thinking that Paul's misgivings about his reception from James and his fellow Brothers were confirmed. That is the kind of information Luke would not want to memorialize—remember how he omitted any mention of Paul's conflict with Peter at Antioch.

Why would the Jerusalem Brothers resent a sizable collection taken up for their benefit? Walther Schmithals argues that James and his fellows were having trouble maintaining their identity against Jews who did not accept Jesus—a hostility that would soon claim the life of James himself. To have Paul's perhaps largely Gentile contingent of uncircumcised Brothers bringing material resources to James could make his position ever more difficult, even untenable. "The Jerusalem church was already then struggling for the last chance of missionary work in Israel. If it accepted Paul's contributions, then it was declaring in the eyes of the Jews its solidarity with him. This threatened to destroy the possibility of its own mission."[1]

Dieter Georgi even suggests that it was Paul's intent to

force the hand of James by an act of deliberate provocation, making James give up his hypocrisy as Peter was challenged to do in Antioch. "The great number of uncircumcised Gentile believers [bringing the collection] was bound to exacerbate the difficulties, tensions, and risks [for James]. The unconditional acceptance of the collection would have constituted a highly compromising step in the eyes of the local Jewish congregation."[2] Georgi suspects that Paul was trying to bring on an eschatological showdown, in which the Jews would be forced to accept the Messiah. This gives the collection for the needy an immense load of possibly catastrophic meaning:

A program of this kind was bound to become a provocation. To judge by Romans 11.11–24, more than being simply aware of this, Paul had made it his declared intent. He hoped that his mission among the Gentiles and their conversion to the Christ faith right in front of the Jews would have the effect of a permanent "irritation" to the Jews, and that the salvation of the latter would eventually result from that irritation. The salvation he had in mind, however, was not one of individual Jews, but one involving the whole world in one universal eschatological miracle (Rom 11.25–36), corresponding in its nature to the collective conversion of the peoples at large, an expectation already present in certain parts of Jewish Scriptures and in certain branches of Judaism. Paul's mission had, therefore, become a symbolic act like the symbolic acts of the biblical prophets. They, too, had often intended to disturb the security Israel derived from the traditonal ideology of salvation. And as was the case with the prophets, so now Paul's provocative thoughts and actions were based heavily on Israelite and Jewish traditions, which would provide the necessary symbolic frame of reference.[3]

But if Paul were going to Jerusalem to trigger the great showdown and end of history, why would he be laying plans to visit Rome and take the revelation to Spain? Besides, he seemed less worried about provoking Jews than about offending James and the Brothers.

It must be admitted, however, that Schmithals and Georgi are right in seeing some deep theological meaning that Paul had invested in the collection for Jerusalem. The nature of that meaning is hard to recover. Paul took his mystery with him into the darkness that descends on his last years. What does seem clear is that his view of things generally was not that of James and the Brothers in Jerusalem, try as he did to effect a reconciliation in his spectacular last journey there. He had been prickly in showing that James had not summoned him earlier, that he went because of "a vision." By contrast, in his last trip, he said he was meeting the obligation incurred in his earlier trip, the agreement to keep in mind the needy. Beyond that, he was repaying the great spiritual debt he and all the Diaspora Jews owed to the original scene of Jesus' redemptive acts.

If we admit some clash between the Jerusalem gatherings and those of the Diaspora, are we not endorsing the view that Paul departed from the original revelation ("gospel") as well as the original scene of Jesus' revelation? We must not fall into some fallacy of firstness here. The easy assumption would be that the Jerusalem gatherings were closer to Jesus' life, death, and meaning than were Brothers in the Diaspora. But remember that our first reports on the gatherings' faith are from Paul. Presence in Jerusalem was no guarantee of fidelity. In fact, the ascendancy of James and the other brothers of the Lord—he had four brothers, including Joseph, Judas, and Simon (Mk 6.3)—after the death of Jesus is a matter for surprise. They had been at odds with Jesus during his lifetime, when "not even his brothers gave him credence" (Jn 7.5). His family, in fact, "tried to take him into custody" (Mk 3.21). Their townspeople tried to throw Jesus over a cliff (Lk 4.29). Jesus was notably cool toward his family members, including his mother (Mk 3.33–35, Lk 11.27–28, Jn 2.4).

If there is any split between Jerusalem and the Pauline gatherings, the real firstness we should look to is Paul's temporal precedence over the Jerusalem reports of Luke. Remember that in the clash with Peter and Barnabas, Barnabas and Paul ended up on the same side (1 Cor 9.6)—as Peter and Paul probably did in their continued Diaspora activity (away from

James), concluding with their deaths in Rome. The genuine meaning of Jesus is to be sought in Paul's revelation, not that of James, in the Diaspora and not in Jerusalem. The Gospels, we should note, were also written in the Diaspora. Few claim, anymore, that they were written in Jerusalem, or even in Judaea.

Luke's Chronology

MUCH OF THE DISPUTE over Luke's account of Paul has to do with his placement of the Jerusalem conference in the chronology of Paul's mission, over which Luke has been the principal (for some the sole) guide. There was for a long time a tendency to save as much as possible of Luke's account, since he was thought to provide the only fixed (nonrelative) date in the whole story. He says that during Paul's first trip to Corinth he was tried in front of the proconsul Gallio (Ac 18.12). An inscription found at Delphi dates Gallio's proconsulship to 51–52 CE. This has been seized on as the pivot on which all other dates could be surmised, as preceding or following the one sure point.

But John Knox noted the ideological usefulness of this point to Luke. By dating the trip to Corinth *after* the Jerusalem encounter, as late as 52 CE, Luke was able to suggest that Paul's preceding work was a kind of apprenticeship under Barnabas, and that Paul's launch out into the fully Gentile world of Europe was done under the aegis of the Jerusalem decree. If this was true, then there was a strange bunching of Paul's extant work and letters *after* 52 CE, a mere decade before his death during which much of his time was (according to Luke himself) spent in prison, while the seventeen years *before* the Jerusalem encounter were comparatively barren of results. And if, on the one hand, Paul's actions and writing were compressed in the last ten years, his collection for Jerusalem must be squeezed into the early part of that time, before his final imprisonments. Knox argues, instead, that when Paul finally went to the Jerusalem "Council," "he had reached the zenith of his career. He had labored in Galatia and Asia, *in Macedonia and Greece*" (emphasis added).[4]

Some try to reduce the problem by trimming the time before the Jerusalem encounter from seventeen to fourteen years. They argue that when Paul said he went first to Jerusalem three years after his calling by Jesus, and then stayed away for fourteen years, he was dating the second period from his calling, not from his first trip to Jerusalem. But if you say that you have gone to a place after three years and then went back after another fourteen, the category remains the same—the time of the visits, not of some preceding event.

Once Knox broke the spell that Luke cast over chronological charts, people began to see many things wrong with the account in Acts. This has led even to skepticism about the one fixed date that everyone relied on, the appearance before Gallio in 51–52 CE. Donald Harman Akenson writes:

> The date is treasured because all the relative chronology of Saul's life suddenly can be hung on a real-world "absolute" date. It is usually cited as the sole absolute dating point in the entire mass of material related to the great Apostle. We want it to be accurate, very, very much. But remember the rule: because of the demonstrable inaccuracy of Acts on many issues on which it can be checked, the grounds of presumption have to be that this event did not take place. Of those events unconfirmed in Saul's letters, it is no different from any other of the events reported in Acts, so no matter how desperately we desire the convenience of an absolute date, it has to be set aside as untrustworthy (again, not necessarily as untrue, but as not commanding trust).[5]

Others see Luke's theological program at work in the Gallio story:

> All of that is much more likely Lukan parable than Pauline history. It is, indeed, Luke's first and most paradigmatic combination of Jewish accusation, Pauline innocence, and Roman dismissal. Look, therefore, at our picture of Corinth's *bema* [tribunal] and see it as a Lukan metaphor for the proper attitude of Rome toward Christianity in

general and as a Lukan symbol of the appropriate response of Rome to Paul in particular. Nothing, however,
in this book presumes the historical actuality of that encounter with Gallio at Corinth or builds the chronological biography of Paul upon its information.[6]

Of course, one need not conclude that Paul was never tried
by Gallio in order to alter Luke's chronology. Paul surely appeared twice in Corinth, probably an intended third time, and
perhaps more (it was a troubled spot much in need of care).
He could have had some judicial moment with Gallio in a later
visit. That would fit with the view of increasing numbers of
scholars who follow Knox's skepticism in questioning Luke's
timetables. They believe Paul took his revelation to Europe
before the Jerusalem encounter that, in Luke's view, validated
it. He no longer has to be seen as receiving his mission to the
nations and then delaying it for seventeen (or fourteen or
whatever) years in order to be blessed by the "apparent leaders" in Jerusalem. These revisions of the old chronology allow
us to recover the original Paul from Luke's sanitized—
"Jerusalemized"—version of his career.

NOTES

1. Walther Schmithals, *Paul and James* (Alec R. Allenson, 1965),
p. 82.

2. Dieter Georgi, *Remembering the Poor: The History of Paul's Collection for Jerusalem* (Abingdon Press, 1992), p. 125.

3. Ibid., p. 118.

4. John Knox, *Chapters in a Life of Paul,* revised edition (Peeters, 1987), p. 40.

5. Donald Harman Akenson, *Saint Saul: A Skeleton Key to the Historical Jesus* (Oxford University Press, 2000), p. 142.

6. John Dominic Crossan and Jonathan L. Reed, *In Search of Paul: How Jesus' Apostle Opposed Rome's Empire with God's Kingdom* (HarperSanFrancisco, 2004), p. 34.

9. Paul and Rome

✝

AFTER PAUL WRITES his Letter to the Romans, we have no more words from him. We must rely on Luke's Acts for his travel to Jerusalem, his treatment there, and his putative final journey toward execution in Rome. The key to the Jerusalem events as presented by Luke is Paul's Roman citizenship. The Jews try to kill him, but he asserts his right as a Roman citizen to be tried in Rome—a dubious right, but just one of many dubious things in Luke's account, including Paul's citizenship. Paul never calls himself a Roman citizen. In fact, he never names a Roman magistrate before whom he appeared. The closest he comes is a reference to one of Rome's client kings, Aretas, whose agent tried to capture him in Damascus (2 Cor 11.32)—Luke's version of that event omits the Roman connection and says simply that the Jews attempted his murder (Ac 9.23–25). The only actual Roman official Paul refers to is a Brother in Rome who had held a provincial office as fund manager (oikonomos) in Corinth (Rom 16.23). Paul was not singling the man out for his rank in this list of those to be greeted in Rome. Since Erastus was a common name, he probably called him "Erastus the fund manager" to distinguish him from other Erastuses.

There are several reasons to doubt Luke's claim that Paul was a Roman citizen. Paul says that he was three times flogged by Roman officials, apart from the five times he was whipped by Jews (2 Cor 11.25)—but flogging Roman citizens was against the law. As Cicero put it in the second trial of Verres (5.66), "It is forbidden to chain a Roman citizen, it is criminal to flog him, it is practically an act of parricide to execute him." Some exceptions to this immunity have been unearthed, but are we to suppose that exceptional circumstances were found for Paul on eight different occasions (presumably in eight different locales)? This would make us conclude not only that the Romans were regularly willing to break their own law, but that the Jews repeatedly risked official anger by flogging a Roman citizen in their synagogues.

The lengths people will go to support Luke's dubious account (in this and many other areas) is shown by Rainer Riesner, who says that Paul might have waived his immunity from flogging in order to be more like Jesus: "Should one not suppose that the apostle, from the perspective of his understanding of the suffering Christ, consciously took such mistreatment upon himself? We should be cautious about precipitately classifying as psychopathological a phenomenon alien to modern secularized Christianity."[1] That Paul, already struggling with epilepsy (or whatever his debilitating "thorn in the flesh" was), would gladly risk his health further when he had missionary work to do is simply unthinkable.

As it turns out, Paul's citizenship backfires on him according to Luke's account. Paul invokes it when Festus, the governor of Caesarea, threatens to send him back to Jerusalem, where the Jews are threatening his life (Ac 25.9). But after Festus refers the matter to Rome, he invites King Agrippa, ruler of the Judaean tetrarchy, to attend a hearing on Paul's presumed offenses. The king is so impressed by Paul that he says, "With a little more persuading you make me a Christian" (26.28). Agrippa then tells Festus privately (how would Luke know this?): "The man could have been freed had he not appealed to the emperor" (26.32). Paul ends up a captive of his own legal "protection."

All Luke's handling of Roman officials is suspect. He artificially arranges for Paul to appear before *four* different tribunals in Jerusalem-Caesarea, where Paul shines and wins sympathy. In one case, the governor's wife is won over by Paul (Ac 24.24). Luke seems to know the story of Pilate's wife sympathizing with Jesus (Mt 27.19), though he did not use it in his own Gospel. At any rate, he draws many parallels between Paul's hearings—before high priests, Sanhedrin, Roman magistrates, and a Herodian king—and Jesus' shuttling back and forth between similar tribunals. It is the same technique Luke had used in creating similarities between Jesus' death and that of Stephen.

Luke, it has been noticed, is as easy on Roman authorities as he is harsh on Jewish ones. He has an almost snobbish interest in officials and wealthy people who are kind to those of the Path, reflecting the need of Luke's churches to cultivate good relations with the Empire. We have also seen that he tries to suppress or soften any clashes between Paul and the Jerusalem Brothers. He not only omitted the blowup between Paul and Peter in Antioch, but offers a strange tale of Paul's reception on his last trip to Jerusalem. Paul had come, remember, to deliver the fund he had collected for the Jewish Brothers. He had feared that James would not receive the offering with grace or favor—and clearly he did not, since Luke has them meet and not even discuss the matter. This was clearly impossible, so whatever happened was so embarrassing to Luke's purpose that he had to excise it from the record. Instead, James is shown warning Paul against Jewish enmities. To disarm that animus, he suggests that Paul should go to the Temple to purify himself (a normal enough procedure after travel in "unclean" countries)—and instead of delivering a fund, proposes that Paul should donate money to some Nazirites (vow takers) for their own purification expenses. This advice, too, backfires, since it is while in the Temple that Paul is seized by Jews who claim he is defiling it. These Jews try Paul and turn him over to the Romans for execution.

This whole matter is fishy. Luke has earlier (Ac 18.18) made Paul himself, during his travels, take a Nazirite vow, letting his hair grow until he had discharged the period of his vow (Hebrew *nazir* means "vow"). Luke does not say why Paul should have done such a thing, and it goes against his whole campaign to make Gentile practice acceptable. Both these vow episodes are totally out of character for Paul, since the Nazirite vow involved the most extreme shunning of "unclean" things (Num 6.2–21), and Paul had written: "I know, relying on the Lord Jesus, that nothing is unclean of itself. Only if a man supposes it unclean does it become unclean for him" (Rom 14.14).

Luke sends Paul off toward Rome, after two years in prison in Caesarea, and has him spend another three months on the island of Malta after a shipwreck. When Paul finally reaches Rome, he is put under house arrest, treated leniently while awaiting trial—and then what? Then nothing. Tradition will say that Paul and Peter, along with a large crowd of Brothers, were killed by Nero as scapegoats for the Roman fire of 64 CE, which destroyed ten of the city's fourteen districts. The tradition has Paul beheaded and Peter crucified, since Paul as a Roman citizen could not be crucified. Actually, the reference to crucifixion in Tacitus's account shows manuscript corruption, and it may have been added by a Christian copyist to accommodate the legend of Peter's death. Tacitus says that Nero's victims were given most "original" *(quaesitissimae)* forms of execution. Tacitus specifies sewing them up in animal skins and letting dogs rend them, or smearing them with pitch and lighting them up at night as garden lamps. Crucifixion was not an "original" form of punishment but a common one. Mention of it does not belong in Tacitus's passage.

It is not surprising that Luke does not want to tell this story. Nero, in effect, destroyed one of Luke's principal theses, that Christians were a peace-loving people who won the respect of Roman authorities. Nero could not have expected to shift blame to the Brothers if they were a respected minority. Tacitus says that Nero made torturing the Brothers a "popular amusement" because the victims were such "foes of human society." But he says something even more damaging to the story of the church's growth that Luke wants to tell. He says that the vast majority of the victims were identified *by informants in their own number*. Apparently the factions that Paul wrote to reconcile—that is, the Jewish Brothers and the Gentile Brothers—had become even more hostile to each other, a development we shall find confirmed in a letter from Clement of Rome. Here is what Tacitus says in his *Annals* (15.44):

Nero, in order to quash the rumor [that he caused the fire himself], found substitute perpetrators and subjected them to the most original forms of execution. These were the ones popularly called Christians, a group hated for its abominations *(flagitia)*. They take their name from a

Christ who was executed by the procurator Pontius Pilate when Tiberius was emperor.

This vile superstition was thus checked for a time but then it broke out again, not only in Judaea, the source of the malady, but in our city, where all that is outlandish or detestable drains in and gets a following. At first the open practitioners were arrested, and by their informing *(indicio eorum)* a vast multitude was taken, not only for setting the fire as for being the foes of human society. Their executions were made a form of public amusement *(ludibria)*, since dogs tore them apart after they were sewn up in animal skins [or they were crucified or flames . . .] or, after nightfall, they were set on fire to serve as lamps. Nero turned over his gardens to these exhibitions and made games of them in the Circus, where he joined the crowd costumed as a charioteer or simply sitting in his chariot—so that, despite the victims' guilt, which merited extreme punishment, there was a reaction of pity, since they seemed to be served up not for the safety of all but for the sadism of one.

That passage could be interpreted to mean that Nero's agents first arrested some Jews who were not Brothers, and that these turned in the Jews who were Brothers. But the best (if indirect) evidence for what happened comes from the aforementioned letter from Clement of Rome. He writes as a scribe for the whole Roman community of Brothers, and the letter is dated to the nineties CE—that is, about three decades after Nero's response to the fire in the city. In Clement's time, the Brothers in Corinth are still engaged in loud internal conflicts, and the Romans write counseling calm and referring to enmities that had earlier rent their own community.

The letter is long and carefully argued, with many proof texts from scripture denouncing strife *(eris)* and division *(stasis)* and calling for mutual forbearance and love. It quotes to the Corinthians what Paul had written to them decades earlier, the praise of love as supreme. It is reasonably supposed that all these arguments were not elaborated just for long-distance advising to another community. They were probably worked out in trying to solve Rome's own problems, including those that led to the deaths of Peter and Paul. They are placed at the climax to a series of "case studies" of the effect of "rivalrous grudges" (the hendiadys *zēlos kai phthonos*). Each of these cases involves betrayal *by one's own*, either one's own family or one's own people, so the deaths of Peter and Paul must involve that too, or there would be no point in the selection of these parallels for them. The carefully wrought passage uses anaphora (repeating *zēlos* at the beginning) to structure the cases:

A *rivalrous* grudge caused the fratricide of Abel by Cain. From *rivalry* father Jacob fled the presence of his brother, Esau. *Rivalry* caused Joseph to be threatened

with death and betrayed into slavery. *Rivalry* forced
Moses to flee Pharaoh's presence when those of his own
blood asked, "Who gave you rule over us—would you
kill us as you slew yesterday the Egyptian?" By *rivalry*
were Aaron and Miriam ostracized from the encamp-
ment. *Rivalry* carried Dathan and Abiram, while still
living, into Hades, since they sowed division *(stasis)*
among the followers of Moses, God's servant. From *rivalry* David suffered not only the foreigners' grudge
(phthonos) but was hounded by Saul, who was Israel's
own king. But enough of ancient cases. Turn we now to
the glorious prize winners *(athlētai)* of recent time; take
we up the model of our own age. From a *rivalrous
grudge* our most prominent and approved pillars were
hounded and they won the prize *(ethlēsan)* of death. Put
we before your gaze our own emissaries. From *rivalry*
Peter suffered not one or two but many ordeals and, offering his life as witness, achieved his merited rank of
honor. From *rivalrous strife* Paul won through to the
trophy for endurance. Though seven times in captivity,
though put to flight, though stoned, this herald of the
faith in both the East and West won a sterling reputation
for his belief, teaching all the world about the right rela-
tionship with God. After he had reached the farthest
term of the West, he offered the authorities the witness
of his life, escaped this world, and entered the sacred
precinct, the very prototype of endurance. (1 Clement,
paragraphs 4–5)

Though it is not said in Luke's Acts, or anywhere else in the New Testament, not even in the pseudo-Pauline letters written years later, that Paul died in Rome, this letter makes that clear—not so much because the gathering that wrote it shows intimate details of the two men's deaths as because it ascribes those deaths to Brothers' "rivalrous grudges"— which meshes perfectly with what Tacitus wrote about the Christian informers in Rome.

The letter gets further confirmation from one written only a few years later, by Ignatius of Antioch. Ignatius, traveling toward Rome, says that he wants to be martyred there and asks the Brothers not to prevent this. He adds to his request this note: "I cannot put you under obligation, as Peter and Paul did. They were emissaries, I am a mere prisoner. They were free, I a slave" (To the Romans, paragraph 4.3). It is interesting that neither Clement nor Ignatius describes Peter and Paul as anything but emissaries. Ignatius is the bishop of Antioch, where he too has been betrayed by Brothers, and he makes much of the bishop's office, addressing the bishop in every other locale he writes a letter to—but to no bishop in Rome. Peter was never the bishop of Rome. Of course, he was a latecomer there, even later than Paul, who did not include him in the Brothers he addressed in the letter to Rome.

It should be noticed that Clement saves Paul for the climactic example in his list of those betrayed, and describes his career far more fully than he does that of Peter. This is not surprising. Paul had a large group of fellow missionaries assembled in Rome by the time he wrote his letter there. If, as Luke indicates, the trip to Jerusalem misfired for Paul, if the fund was not well received, if the Jews (whether Brothers or not) caused him trouble and delayed his arriving in Rome for years, then the Pauline team would have had time to organize and proselytize, gaining new recruits for their project. This probably had something to do with the fact that Tacitus can refer to a vast multitude *(multitudo ingens)* of believers caught in his dragnet of victims. It should be remembered, too, that a minority informed on this majority. That would fit with the idea that the returning Jewish Brothers found a thriving Gentile Brothers community in place after the six years of exile under Claudius—not to mention that a devoted group of Paul's followers had entered the situation and extended its influence while he was gone. Paul and Peter were both members of the betrayed party—themselves Jewish Brothers, they would have stood with the Gentile Brothers, as befits their status as emissaries in the Diaspora.

Clement seems to tell us something more about Paul. Luke says he went to Rome and was under house arrest, presumably to stand trial for some charge Festus sent ahead with him—Luke suggests no charge more specific than causing trouble among Jerusalem's Jews. Clement does not indicate that Paul was killed because of any legal proceeding that originated in Jerusalem. He tells us something far more interesting—that Paul taught "all the world" after "he had reached the farthest term of the West." This indicates that he did in fact lead his mission team to Spain, after the Jerusalem case against him failed.

Legend says that James, one of the Twelve, was the emissary who took the faith to Spain, but it is far more likely, and more fitting, to think that Paul did it, that his careful plan to go there with a team of missionaries was finally carried out, despite many intervening obstacles. But if that is the case, why do no further letters tell us of this mission? The troubles in Rome may have called Paul back, and anything he wrote about those troubles was too sad or disheartening to be preserved. *Nothing* direct is preserved on the believers' side of the final disgrace of internal division in Rome and the death of the two greatest emissaries there. The only direct evidence is that of the pagan Tacitus. Clement and Ignatius give us only indirect (discreet) evidence. The most plausible guess about what happened is that Paul came back to deal with the conflicts between the Brothers, and fell as one of the victims of the informers' dirty work with Nero. If this is the case, then he followed his divine master in one final respect. They were both killed by religion.

Clement chimes with Tacitus, as well, in saying that Peter underwent "not one or two but many ordeals" and that Paul "won through to the trophy of endurance." This may be the Roman community's uneasy way of remembering the "original forms of execution" Nero invented as a public amusement. If the two great emissaries died under Nero, then Peter was not crucified, either upside down or right side up, and the citizen status Luke foisted on Paul had nothing to do with his death. They probably died in one of the obscene ways Tacitus describes, torn apart in animal costumes or serving as ornamental torches in Nero's garden. This was not an end Luke could bring himself to set down. One comfort is to realize that Peter and Paul, who had clashed bitterly in Antioch, died as comrades.

We have no description of their bearing at the end. But it is safe to think that Paul, who had not been cowed or deterred by endless sufferings, from the thorn in his flesh, from shipwrecks, from floggings, from imprisonments, was not one to flinch from the last blow. He had earlier said that he wanted to die and be with the risen Jesus, the God he had seen directly. With that as a stay, he would not waver: "I have learned self-reliance in any situation. I know how to get along with little or with a lot. Experience has given me an edge over any or all turns, to cope with fullness or hunger, with surplus or deprivation. I am up to any test so long as he gives me strength for it" (Phil 4.11–13).

We do not know what his last words were. But his last words for us, the ones we may well turn to as we face our own final test, are these:

God with us, who is to oppose? If he spared not his own Son, but gave him up for us all, how can every other favor not be given with that one? Who can reject the ones he chooses? Where God vindicates, who can incriminate? The dead man is Messiah—say rather the risen man, now at God's right hand, and taking our cause. What, then, can sunder us from the Messiah's love? Will dire straits, impasse, persecution, starvation, nakedness, peril, or the sword? Scripture says, "We are dying for you all day, nothing but sheep to be cut down," yet in every way we win the victory because of the one who loves us. I am firmly convinced that neither death nor life, neither angels nor supremacies, neither present nor future force, not what is already or what will be, not any powers, no high thing, no low thing, not some other frame of things, can keep us away from the love of God that is in Messiah-Jesus, our Lord. (Rom 8.31–39)

NOTE

1. Rainer Riesner, *Paul's Early Period,* translated by Doug Stott (Eerdmans, 1998), p. 150.

Afterword: Misreading Paul

☩

IT IS NOT HARD to see why Bernard Shaw thought the world would have been better off had Paul never lived. Consider, out of many cases illustrating this, one typically bleak Pauline moment in history, from the history of the Massachusetts Bay Colony. Anne Hutchinson crossed the Atlantic to follow a vision hatched from Paul's Letter to the Romans. She was seeking a "justification" that would free her from her own dark and baffled quest for virtue. She knew only one pastor who could assuage her longing, John Cotton, and he had left England for Boston. She, with her husband and children, followed Cotton in 1633. She championed Cotton against all the other ministers of New England.

He had taught her an extreme version of what Luther took from Paul (Rom 3.20), that observing "the works of the law" avails not at all toward "justification." She took this to mean that any pastors urging people to do virtuous deeds were preaching "a covenant of works" that undermined the real Gospel (the covenant of grace). She engaged in competitive helplessnesses so far as all human effort was concerned. To do this, she gathered a group of women in her home to correct what they were hearing in church. These women were gradually joined by some of their husbands or male relatives. When Cotton became leery of where she was taking his teaching, she came to believe that only she was true to the real covenant of grace. Her flaunted helplessness became a self-confidence that she could lay down the law for everyone else, because it was not she but the Spirit within her that was speaking—an arrogance that often issues from Pauline "humility."

The male authorities of church and state in Boston fought genuine Pauline teaching (however misunderstood) with pseudo-Pauline strictures (understood all too domineeringly well). They invoked against her the letter of "Paul" saying, "I forbid a woman to teach" (1 Tim 2.12). She countered from another pseudo-Pauline letter, to Titus (Tit 2.4), saying the older women should teach the younger. But her accusers caught her up on what the elders were to teach their young sisters—"to be submissive to their husbands" (Tit 2.5). She was teaching men, not women, and teaching them contempt for their pastors. She could not win any game where "Paul" could trump Paul. It is hard to tell which was the more blighting influence, real Paul or fake Paul, in this exchange—or in any of thousands of transactions where the ability to use Paul for dark purposes has been evident.

The heart of the problem is this. Paul entered the bloodstream of Western civilization mainly through one artery, the vein carrying a consciousness of sin, of guilt, of the tortured conscience. This is the Paul we came to know through the brilliant self-examinations of Augustine and Luther, of Calvin and Pascal and Kierkegaard. The profound writings of these men and their followers, with all their vast influence, amount to a massive misreading of Paul, to a historic misleading of the minds of the minds of people down through the centuries—or so goes the argument of Bishop Krister Stendahl. In 1961 Stendahl gave a short but incisive lecture to the American Psychological Association, a work he called "The Apostle Paul and the Introspective Conscience of the West."[1] He argues that Luther and his followers took Paul's argument for freedom from the externals of the Mosaic code as a confession of his own inability to follow moral law in general. They read as autobiography Paul's exclamation at Romans 7.22–24: "In my inner self, I am pleased with God's Law. But I observe another law in my limbs doing battle with the law in my mind, holding me prisoner to the law of sin in my limbs. Miserable person that I am, who is to set me free from this body doomed to death?" These words have echoed thunderously in the depths of generations for whom they are an autobiographical outcry.

But Stendahl notices an odd thing. In all of Paul's undoubtedly autobiographical references, there is no expression of guilt. Far from finding it hard to observe the Mosaic Law, he says that he observed it perfectly in his days as a Pharisee (Phil 3.6), and in his days among the Brothers he says repeatedly that he has done nothing for which his conscience could reproach him (1 Cor 4.4, 2 Cor 1.12, Rom 9.1). In fact, says Stendahl, Paul manifests a "robust conscience," not a guilty one. What sets him so at odds with his dark interpreters, and what does their favorite passage mean? How could this one place be so at odds with what he tells us about himself in other places?

Stendahl gives us the obvious answer. In this one place *he is not telling us about himself*. The Romans passage is part of a complex interplay of "persons" in diatribe-exchanges, meant to show that Gentiles and Jews—not as individuals but as societies—have both failed to observe their covenant with God. Pagans, given the natural law, became unnatural. Jews, given covenant law, repeatedly rebelled against it. The Jewish diatribal figure is speaking in the passage at Romans 7.22–24. Paul is arguing that neither side can reproach the other, and that God is on neither side. Modern exegetes—for instance, Wayne Meeks—emphasize this as the whole point of the Letter to the Romans, where Paul was addressing the divisions between Gentile Brothers and Jewish Brothers.[2]

Paul was speaking of God as the savior of whole peoples. American black religion was closer to him than have been individualist members of intellectual elites. The blacks spoke of the whole people being delivered from Pharaoh, or reaching the Holy Land, or surviving the Ark's passage. Luther reflects a brilliant but hypertrophic blending of late medieval penitential disciplines and the Renaissance's subjective individualism.

This speaks to us at a very intimate level because we are a part of the world created by those trends. But Paul was entirely innocent of such cultures.

If we ask why Paul has come down to us as the Bad News Man, we have to remember the wisdom of Lucretius (1.101):

> *Tantum religio potuit suadere malorum.*
> How suasive is religion to our bane.

Religion took over the legacy of Paul as it did that of Jesus—because they both opposed it. They said that the worship of God is a matter of interior love, not based on external observances, on temples or churches, on hierarchies or priesthoods. Both were at odds with those who impose the burdens of "religion" and punish those who try to escape them. They were radical egalitarians, though in ways that delved below and soared above conventional politics. They were on the side of the poor, and saw through the rich. They saw only two basic moral duties, love of God and love of the neighbor. Both were liberators, not imprisoners—so they were imprisoned. So they were killed. Paul meant what Jesus meant, that love is the only law. Paul's message to us is not one of guilt and dark constraint. It is this:

Finally, Brothers, whatever things are true, whatever honorable, whatever making for the right, whatever lovable, whatever admirable—if there is any virtue, any-thing of high esteem—think on these. All you have learned, have taken from tradition, have listened to, have observed in me, act on these, and the God who brings peace will be yours. (Phil 4.8–9)

NOTES

1. Stendahl's lecture is reprinted in *Paul Among Jews and Gentiles* (Fortress Press, 1976).

2. Wayne Meeks, "Judgment and the Brother: Romans 14.1–15.13," in Gerald F. Hawthorne, editor, *Tradition and Interpretation in the New Testament* (Eerdmans 1987), pp. 290–300.

Appendix: Translating Paul

KRISTER STENDAHL AND JOHN GAGER both tell us that modern translations, even those that seem most "objective," distort what Paul was saying. Paul's writings are the first to reach us from a follower of Jesus. It is hard to avoid anachronism when we try to reenter Paul's world—to avoid terms that did not exist for Paul, terms like *Christian, church, priests, sacraments, conversion.* All such terms subtly, or not so subtly, pervert what was being said in its original situation. Even a direct transliteration like *apostle* can be misleading. These poor translations come with heavy suggestions of later developments, giving Paul an atmosphere of "religion," a thing he opposed. To scrub away linguistic accretions on Paul's text is as necessary as to cleanse away the buildup of foreign matter on old paintings. Only by doing this can we travel back into the Spirit-haunted, God-driven world of Paul in the heady first charismatic days of Jesus' revelation.

Below I list first the customary translation, then the Greek term, then a more adequate rendering. I use the last terms for translating Paul throughout this book.

"Christians" *(Adelphoi)*
Brothers

The term *Christian* was first used by pagan opponents of Christianity—by Pliny the Younger, for instance, or Tacitus, or Lucian. Religious groups often end up being called by names that were initially derisory—Jesuits, Lollards ("Mumblers"), Puritans, Quakers, Shakers, Ranters, Diggers, Mormons, and so on. Luke in the Acts of the Apostles (Ac 11.26) says that the followers of Jesus were first called Christians at Antioch, but neither he nor Paul uses it of their fellows in faith. King Agrippa is the only person quoted by Luke as referring to a Christian (Ac 26.2). People we now call Christians had a number of expressions for each other, stressing their affective bonds. There are so many terms precisely because *Christian* had not yet been accepted, to absorb them all.

1. Brothers *(Adelphoi):* This is the normal term, both in Paul and Luke, for the followers of Jesus. In the short First Letter to the Thessalonians, Paul uses it twelve times in direct address and three times in description. Though the masculine noun was used generically for the whole Brotherhood, Paul addressses specific women followers of Jesus as Sister *(Adelphē)*—the wives of Peter and the Lord's brothers, for instance (1 Cor 9.5), or Phoebe (Rom 16.1) or Apphia (Phlm 2). And when he distinguishes between male and female duties, he refers

to what should be done by "the Brother or the Sister" (1 Cor 7.15).

2. The Holy *(Hagioi,* or *Hēgiasmenoi):* Paul also refers to "the Holy" in such-or-such a place, or to "the needs of the Holy" (Rom 12.13). They were the Holy because they had been incorporated into Jesus by baptism: "For just as one body has many members, and all the members make up that single body, so, in Christ we became one body by baptism, through the action of a single Spirit, whether we be Jews or Greeks, slaves or free, all were given to drink of the one Spirit" (1 Cor 12.12–13).

3. Those in Messiah *(Hoi en Christō[i]):* Because they are baptized into Jesus, the Holy can be said to be "in Jesus"—or in Messiah-Jesus or in Jesus-Messiah. Thus Paul can say, "I was not known by my features to the Judaean gatherings in Messiah" (Gal 1.22). Or similarly: "Anyone in Messiah is a new order of being" *(ktisis,* 2 Cor 5.17).

4. The Called *(Klētoi):* Paul thinks of the Brothers as summoned to holiness (Rom 1.6, 8.28, 1 Cor 1.24).

5. Housefellows *(Oikeioi):* Since the followers met mainly in each other's homes *(oikoi),* Paul calls them, in general, housefellows of our trust (Gal 6.10, Eph 2.19).

6. Those of the Path *(Hoi tēs Hodou):* This term has become common by the time of the Acts of the Apostles. Luke therefore can speak of detractors or persecutors of

the Path (Ac 22.4), of debating or understanding the Path (19.23, 24.22).

"Christ" (Khristos)
Messiah

One reason Paul did not use the term *Christian* is that *Christ* was not a proper name for him. "Jesus Christ" was not praenomen-cognomen, any more than was "Jesus Lord." *Khristos* is, like *Kyrios* (Lord), a title. It is simply the Greek word for *Messiah*. They both mean "Anointed," with the same theological sense. It is essential to keep in mind that the full Jewish force of the title was always important for Paul, since he always thinks of Jesus as fulfilling Jewish Law and prophecy. Paul sometimes uses the word with the article—*the* Messiah—sometimes without (not on any regular plan). He uses it with the name of Jesus, either as Messiah-Jesus or Jesus-Messiah, but in all cases it is the title that is at issue, as N. T. Wright has properly emphasized.[1]

"Church" (Ekklēsia)
Gathering

The Greek *ekklēsia* simply means "gathering." The meeting place of the Brothers was almost always in Paul's time the house of a Brother or a Sister, or both—as in "the gathering at Prisca's and Aquila's house" (1 Cor 16.19, Rom 16.5) or "the gathering at your [Philemon's] house" (Phlm 2). So basic is this cell of the Brothers' assembly that Paul could refer, as we have seen, to all the Brotherhood as "the housefellows *(oikeioi)* of our trust" (Gal 6.10). Some towns or regions had two or more such gathering spots—like "the gatherings in Macedonia" (2 Cor 8.1) or "the gatherings in Galatia" (Gal 1.2)—with no hierarchy among them. All those in one city could be called, for instance, "God's gathering at Corinth" (1 Cor 1.2, 2 Cor 1.1). What would later be called "the church" is, for Paul, "all the gatherings" (1 Cor 4.17, 7.17, 14.33), "God's gatherings" (1 Cor 11.16), or simply "God's gathering" (1 Cor 10.32, 11.22, 15.9), or "the gathering" (1 Cor 12.28).

"Gospel" *(Euaggelion)*
Revelation

The gospel is what Paul is told to take to the nations. It is so central to his vocation that he uses it as a verb—he must be "gospeling." He talks indeed of "the gospel I gospeled to you . . . in the sense in which I gospeled it to you" (1 Cor 15.1–2). What precisely does that mean? We are somewhat confused by the fact that later compositions, the four Gospels, are now equated with "the gospel." Yet giving the etymology ("favorable announcement') is not translating, either. That would make Paul speak of "the favorable announcement I favorably announced to you." For Paul as an emissary carrying a message, the gospel is the *revelation* that Jesus died for our sins and rose again, and this is the entire meaning of history, it is what God wants to reveal about himself.

So "the gospel I gospeled to you" is "the revelation I revealed to you," and Paul warns against those who would "gospel against what I gospeled"—that is, who reveal something at odds with what he revealed (Gal 1.8). Such people "were not hewing to the clearly marked meaning of the revelation" (Gal 2.14). The revelation is not only something that Paul and his coworkers carry to others, but what they "serve" (Phlm 13). It has its own power: "The revelation was not brought to you in words only but in miracle and the Holy Spirit" (1 Thess 1.5).

"Preach" *(Euaggelizein)*
Bring the Revelation

Other New Testament authors use *kērysso* ("proclaim") for preaching, but Paul uses that verb only six times, and two of them are for dubious proclamations (Gal 5.11, Rom 2.21). Overwhelmingly the word usually translated as "preach" is the verb from *euaggelizo*. This has the meaning of God's still actively revealing his plans. Paul even "does priestly service" *(hierourgōn)* to this revelation (Rom 15.16). Paul never uses the word for priest *(hiereus)*, since no such office existed among the Brothers. Priesthood in the Jewish tradition had to do with the offering of animal sacrifice, and later Christians would import that meaning into their use of the term. In the New Testament, Jesus is the only individual called a priest, in the late anonymous Letter to the Hebrews. Paul in Romans uses "priestly service to the revelation" to suggest coming out from behind the Temple veils: "The revelation *(euaggelion)* I brought you proclaiming Jesus-Messiah unveils the secret kept hidden through the ages, but now brought forth as confirmed by the prophets in the order appointed by the ageless God for all nations to recognize with an acknowledging trust" (Rom 16.25). "Scripture made a prior revelation [literally pregospeled, *pro-eueggelisato*] of this to Abraham" (Gal 3.8). The revelation in Paul has its own divine power, so he speaks of "when the revelation first began to work" (Phil 4.15). As usual, God is acting directly through Paul.

"Faith" *(Pistis)*

Trust

We normally think of our faith as having faith *(pistis)* in God. But Paul talks of God having faith *(pistis)*. What is God's faith in? In himself? In his own words? In us? The last might seem the least plausible. How can he believe in us? But this problem reveals the inadequacy of our sense of trust. God takes us into his trust. There is no longer an estrangement. He promotes us into a partnership with him because we are members of his Son's mystical body. We trust him as sons. He trusts us as a father trusts his beloved children. This explains the difficult passage at Romans 1.17, "from *pistis* to *pistis.*" If we already have trust, how do we move to get it? But if one of these is God's *pistis,* the passage makes sense: "God's vindication is unveiled, from [his] trust to [our] trust, it is written: 'The vindicated will live from trust.'" Too often faith now means belief in a proposition, a dogma, the stand taken by a church. It is, instead, an active response to a *Person,* a trust in him.

"Justification" *(Dikiuosynē)*

Vindication

The verb *dikaoiun* means "to set things right." In means to uphold the law. When God is *dikaios* he is upholding his law. When we are *dikaioi* we are upheld by law. Does that mean that we are innocent, or acquitted, or both? In any case we are vindicated, our title is made clear. Paul says that God is our vindicator. That is why we trust him. The initiative is his. When Paul says, "Abraham was vindicated by trusting God" (Rom 4.2–3), he is not saying that he won vindication but that he accepted what God told him with trust. When God is said to have been "vindicated in what you said, and proved innocent in what you did" (Rom 3.4), it is not because he can be put on trial, but because he can vindicate his claims by his power, by manifesting it. In the same way, when we pray in the Our Father "Your name be made holy" (Mt 6.9), *we* cannot make it holy. No human being can. We are praying that

God vindicate his title (name) by manifesting it. In the same way, he vindicates *our* title when he makes us holy, out of his munificence uniting us with his Son, making "Messiah-Jesus our vindication" (*dikaiosyne*, 1 Cor 1.30). In fact, Jesus makes us "God's vindication" (2 Cor 5.21).

Luther tried to separate "justification" from "works," in a sterile way. When we trust God, we gladly keep our part of the covenant with him. Luther wanted to excise from the New Testament canon the Letter of James 2.20, "Trust without action is feckless," but he would have to pare away many authentic parts of the Pauline corpus to deny the same basic point—for instance: "All you have learned, have taken from tradition, have listened to, have observed in me, *act* on these" (Phil 4.9). Speaking to the Corinthians on their good works for the Jerusalem fund, he says, "God will make fertile the effects of your vindication" (2 Cor 9.10). "Good works" were hardly scorned by Paul.

"Be Converted" *(Klēthēnai)*
Be Summoned

When it is said that Paul became a Christian, or was converted to Christianity, this offers a polar expression that implies that he converted from Judaism to Christianity. Paul did not think of himself as being converted from Judaism, and there was no such thing as Christianity, or a Christian church, for him to join. He converted others to the Jewish God,

Yahweh, but he did not need to be converted to Yahweh himself. He taught non-Jews from the Jewish scripture (the only "Bible" that existed in his time), saying they must become part of the "seed of Abraham," inheritors of the Jewish covenant that had been extended to them *without having been canceled for the Jews.* He always spoke of himself as a Jew, spoke of "my people," of the people of Abraham.

If Paul was not converted, neither did he convert others. The normal words for conversion, *metanoein* ("repent" or "rethink") and *epistrephein* ("turn back"), were used, in the Septuagint, for prophets recalling Jews to the covenant that they were neglecting. John the Baptist issues a call for *metanoia* in the Gospels (Mk 1.15, for instance). But when Paul uses such language, it is usually in a negative sense, when he tells Gentiles *not* to "turn back" *(epistrephein)* to idols (Gal 4.9) after they had once turned from idols (1 Thess 1.9); when he rebukes the Corinthians for *not* rethinking *(metanoesantes)* their return to sinful ways (2 Cor 12.21); or when he quotes the Septuagint (2 Cor 3.16). What people call Paul's "conversion" was his reception of a vocation, of a call—to carry the revelation (gospel) to the nations. He did not ask the Gentiles to be "converted" but to receive *their* call. For him God always takes the initiative toward humankind. Paul asks not that people know God but that they be known by him (Gal 4.9), that they be his chosen ones *(eklektoi)*, his called ones *(klētoi)*, his summoned ones *(klēthentes)*, the ones he made holy *(hagioi)*. God is always the dynamic principle for Paul.

"Salvation" *(Sotēria)*
Rescue

The revelation is that all the nations, not merely the Jews, are to be "saved" *(sōzesthai)*. "Salvation" has become something we think of as a condition of the individual, something he or she gains, loses, or feels sure of ("Brother, are you saved?"). This reflects the introspective individualism Krister Stendahl calls a deflection of Paul's message. Paul did not think of the person's own sense of himself, but of God's activity as the rescuer. Rescue was for him a divine initiative, God's raid on enemy territory, bringing the people out from captivity. As black Americans think of the whole people as escaping Pharaoh or reaching the Promised Land, so the whole of creation is to be rescued and restored to God.

The very frame of things is giddy with apprehension at what will be unveiled for the sons of God. The frame of things has been baffled, despite itself, by the one constraining it—yet with hope for it, since the whole frame will be liberated from its imprisoning decay, freed into the splendor of God's offspring. All the frame of things, we realize, has been moaning in the throes of some birth—and we, moreover, though we have the first harvest of the Spirit, moan along with it, yearning for full adoption as heirs and for the release of our bodies. (Rom 8.19–23)

We might wonder how Paul, who expected the consummation of the world to be completed soon, thought he could, in effect, convert persons one by one throughout the world. But he did not see God working retail. He was moving a great cosmic plan forward.

God initiates it all by rejoining us to himself through Messiah and by making us active in this rejoining—as we profess that God is rejoining the world to himself through Messiah, not counting their lapses against them, entrusting to us the message of this rejoining. This makes us Messiah's ambassadors, as God issues his call to you through us. We implore you, then, to be rejoined to Messiah. The one who was innocent of sin he treated as sin for our sakes, to make us in him the vindication of God. (2 Cor 5.18–21)

"Redemption" *(Apolytrōsis)*
Release

Apolytrōsis means, literally, "ransom." But its translation into Latin *redemptio*, "buying back," has been caught up into Anselm's notions of paying off God the Father by sacrifice of his Son, a concept foreign to Paul. Paul means by the ransoming of the whole world a release of it from thralldom to the evil order he personified as Satan. It is a massive liberation act, like the breaking open of every prison, and only God's energy can accomplish this.

"Grace" *(Charis)*
Favor

"Grace," too, has acquired foreign associations through the history of the churches. It is often thought of as a quantum acquired by an individual, as something one gains or loses. To be "in grace," or deprived of grace, is like having or losing gas in one's spiritual tank. Once again, the introspective individual has got in the way of Paul's thinking. Grace is God's gratuitous activity, his favor, his bounty, in a continuing dynamic activity on his part.

"Apostle" *(Apostolos)*
Emissary

The Greek *apo-stolos*, from *apo-stello*, means one "sent off." It is used of an emissary, and in Paul's time it meant a messenger from or to the gatherings—or, in Paul's special vocation, "an emissary to the nations" (Gal 2.8, Rom 11.13). Paul gives, as a synonym for "emissary," "ambassador" (2 Cor 5.20). This was not an office but a function (like the other ministries of Paul's time). One became an emissary by being sent off from one body or mission to another—either by election (2 Cor 8.19, 23) or by appointment, as when Paul dispatches an assistant to one of the gatherings (1 Thess 3.2, 1 Cor 4.17, 2 Cor 8.18, 22, 9.13).

The misunderstanding of this term comes from trying to turn it from a function to an office, and a ruling office at that. Most often we hear of "the twelve apostles"—or thirteen if we add Paul. "The Twelve" do have an office in the Gospels, an eschatological one—they are symbolic judges of the end time, to sit on the seats of the Twelve Tribes (Mt 19.28, Lk 22.30). But they are usually just "the Twelve" in the Gospels, or the twelve followers (mathētai). They are referred to as "twelve emissaries" (apostoloi) when they are "sent off" on a mission to Judaean villages (Mt 10.1–8)—that is, when they exercise the technical function of emissaries. They are never rulers of any gathering. The leader of the Jerusalem church was James the brother of the Lord, who was not a member of the Twelve. Peter is an emissary in the strict sense because he goes as an emissary into the Diaspora, to Lydda, Joppa, Caesarea, and Antioch (Ac 9.32, 10.18, Gal 2.7–10–11)—and eventually to Rome. The later tradition that restricts apostles to the Twelve is not something Paul knew. He says that the risen Jesus appeared to the Twelve and afterward to "all the emissaries" (1 Cor 15.5–7). Those are distinct groups. That is why he can refer to his fellow emissaries, like Andronicus and Junia (Rom 16.7), or to "emissaries" as a regular part of the gatherings (1 Cor 12.28).

"Bishop" (Episkopos)

Overseer

Paul uses the word *episkopoi* ("overseers") only once, when he greets the Holy in Philippi (Phil 1.1), "along with their overseers and attendants *(diakonoi)*." These are informal leaders who have nothing in common with the later *bishops* and *deacons* of the church. The plural and mixed "overseers" referred to are not the single-rule *(monarchoi)* bishops that arose half a century later in the time of Ignatius, and the "attendants" are not the seven supply managers elected in Jerusalem according to Luke (Ac 6.1–6). *Attendants* is such a general term with Paul that he can refer to Satan's attendants (2 Cor 11.15), to his foes in Corinth as so-called attendants on Messiah (2 Cor 11.23), to Jesus himself as an attendant on the circumcision (Rom 15.8), as well as to himself and his team as attendants on God (2 Cor 6.4) and on the new covenant (2 Cor 3.6). Those who try to make *diakonos* mean the later "deacon" are embarrassed by the fact that Phoebe is a *diakonos* (Rom 16.1). Paul is not referring to a ruling structure under any of these titles, since the gatherings are still charismatic groups where the Spirit singles out people for their function, not their office. These include a wide variety of gifts—emissaries, prophets, teachers, healers, readers, miracle workers, guides, speakers in tongues, interpreters of tongues, wise men, spirit testers, trainers, attendants, exhorters, distributors, patrons, almsgivers, shepherds (1 Cor 4.15, 12.8–10,

27–28, Rom 11.6–8). None of these are ruling roles, and "overseers" make only one fleeting reference among them. "Priests" make no appearance at all.

NOTE

1. N. T. Wright, *The Climax of the Covenant* (Fortress Press, 1993), pp. 41–55.

Acknowledgments

MY EDITOR at Viking, Carolyn Carlson, had the idea for my preceding book *What Jesus Meant,* so she must take the blame for this companion volume. Martin Marty read the whole manuscript and made valuable suggestions improving it. My agent, Andrew Wylie, undergirds it all. The final arbiter, as always, is my own special Italian tempest and solace, Natalie.

Printed in the United States
by Baker & Taylor Publisher Services